Thy Kingdom Come

STERLING W. SILL

Wherefore, may the kingdom of God go forth, that the kingdom of heaven may come, that thou, O God, mayest be glorified in heaven so on earth, that thine enemies may be subdued; for thine is the honor, power and glory, forever and ever. Amen.
(*D&C 65:6.*)

Thy Kingdom Come

Sterling W. Sill

Published by
Deseret Book Company
Salt Lake City, Utah
1975

Contents

Section 4
Learning and Leading

Section 5
Our Goal: Eternal Life

Preface

Charles Dickens is regarded by many people as being the greatest English novelist of all time. He possessed a great abundance of creative energy and left a large number of delightful and worthwhile writings for us to think about.

He began one of his best-known books, *A Tale of Two Cities,* by describing that period immediately preceding the French Revolution, saying:

"It was the best of times, it was the worst of times, it was the age of wisdom, it was the age of foolishness, it was the epoch of belief, it was the epoch of incredulity, it was the season of Light, it was the season of Darkness, it was the spring of hope, it was the winter of despair, we had everything before us, we had nothing before us, we were all going direct to Heaven, we were all going direct the other way."

With some accuracy, Mr. Dickens was describing an important condition of contrasts that exists in our world. It applied not only to the period preceding the French Revolution; it applies even more significantly to our own time.

The apostle Paul also looked down to our day and referred to it as the dispensation of the fulness of times when all things would be brought together in one. Our day is certainly not a time of minimums. There is a condition in the world that sometimes tends to keep the balance even between the negative and positive influences. And during the period of the increases in our standards of living, our education, and our opportunities, we also have had a corresponding increase in crime, lethargy, and the number and intensity of our sins. It is expected that to the very end of our earth's existence as we know it, this design of contrasts and opposites will continue.

In one of the important modern-day revelations, the Lord referred to the Word of Wisdom as being adapted to the capacity of the weak and the weakest of all Saints, who are or can be called Saints. That condition should make our greatest success easy, yet we hear from many people how impossible it is, in their opinion, for them to live their religion. We hear till we are weary about the temptations of our day, and the seemingly universal appeal of evil is indicated by the numerous cries that "everybody is doing it." However, it is interesting that no temptation is a temptation at all unless we ourselves are personally entertaining it. God never forces anyone to do right, and Satan has no power to force anyone to do wrong.

Someone put this idea in verse when he said:

All the water in the world
However hard it tried
Could never sink the smallest ship
Unless it got inside,
And all the evil in the world,
The blackest kind of sin,
Can never hurt you the least bit
Unless you let it in.

Jesus himself gave a stimulating picture of that straight and narrow way which leads to all good things, as compared with the broad, unpleasant, meandering course that ends with misery and death. From the very beginning of time, it has seemed that the straight path that leads to eternal life is rather sparcely traveled, whereas the broad road that leads to death is still attracting great numbers of travelers. One of the serious tragedies of our day is that so many people are missing the main targets of life by shooting under them, just as they did in the days of ancient Babylon, Greece and Rome, Sodom and Gomorrah. In the meridian of time, our world's inhabitants made their most serious mistake by crucifying the Son of God, who came to the earth to work in their interests.

This low view of life is still with us and still seems to be more popular than the high view. We still seem to prefer to walk through the low marshy swamplands of existence rather than along the mountaintops of success. However, we may be sure that the most profitable purpose in life is righteousness. The most sought-after employees are those who are honest, moral, industrious, and faithful. The happiest families are those that follow most closely the teachings of the Savior of the world. The greatest businessmen are those who follow the teachings of the Master.

We may each focus our lives in any direction. God was pointing upward and forward when he said such things as "Ye are gods; and all of you are children of the most High." (Psalm 82:6.) Jesus said to us, "Be ye therefore perfect, even as your Father which is in heaven is perfect" (Matthew 5:48); "be ye doers of the word, and not hearers only" (James 1:22); "be of good cheer" (John 16:33); "be not afraid" (Matthew 14:27). It is made perfectly clear in the scriptures that if we follow that straight and narrow path described by the Master, then as the offspring of God, we may sometime hope to become like our eternal heavenly parents. This doctrine of exaltation, despite its wonder and glory, has always seemed to be difficult for people to accept. For some reason, we seem to favor those philosophies which minimize our destiny, and we spend far too much of our time doing those things which tend to bring misery and death upon ourselves.

The most tragic example of this view is Lucifer, who fell from heaven to become Satan, the father of lies, the father of immoralities, the father of crime, and the father of unhappiness. The scriptures mention many groups who followed him. Of one of these groups, it was said that they love Satan more than God. They tend to love immorality more than purity; ugliness more than beauty. Solomon said, "Where there is no vision, the people perish. . . ." (Proverbs 29:18.) He might also have said that where there is no study, no contemplation, no character control, there is no vision. When we allow our lack of knowledge or our poor judgment to produce weakness and failure in us, we begin to follow the low road where we have an unprofitable and distorted view of life's benefits. When we seriously lack understanding and the spirit of the gospel, we fill our lives with weakness, failure, and despair, placing the most serious handicaps upon us.

When each of us has reached the full stature of his development by his own faith, integrity, and works, then the greatest good in the world will be accomplished. It is hoped that some of the chapters that follow will stimulate our thinking so that they will not only help us do our work, but will also help us to help the Lord do his work.

*"Thy kingdom is an everlasting
kingdom, and thy dominion endureth
throughout all generations."*
(*Psalm 145:13.*)

Identifying
The Kingdom

1
Thy Kingdom Come

The other day, I heard a fine discourse by a wise mother in which she explained some ways in which she was trying to make her family's home into a kind of forerunner and prototype of what she sometime expected her heavenly home to be. The way to become a great soul in heaven is to practice being a great soul here, and doing those things that make us genuinely happy now helps insure our greatest happiness for later on.

This life is primarily a build-up and rehearsal for eternity, and this woman's thesis is perfectly logical that her home here will in many ways be the forerunner of her eternal home. God intended that life itself should be a schoolmaster to provide us with experiences for that important period that lies beyond the boundaries of this life. It is primarily a preparation for eternity. Our most serious tragedy would come about if by our disobedience and sin we were to fall in the exalted purposes, which would tend to make our homes prototypes of hell rather than tastes of heaven.

The creation of man is not something that was finished in the Garden of Eden six thousand years ago. The creation of man is still going on. To some degree, it took place in our own homes last week, and it will take place there again next month, and we ourselves are the creators. That is, we are creating the characters, the personalities, and the faith that will determine what our lives are going to be throughout eternity. We are also going to have a hand in determining the future of the earth itself, which, when it is cleansed and exalted, will serve as the heavenly home of those who qualify for celestial glory.

There has always been a vital relationship between our great earth and those of us who live upon it. When our first parents disobeyed God by partaking of the forbidden fruit, their sin brought mortality upon themselves, but it also brought a downward change upon the earth, which was lowered to a telestial state. Just as we share with God the responsibility for our own creation, so we also share with him the responsibility for the redemption and glorification of the earth. By everything that we do, we are either helping or hindering him in his work of salvation and redemption. As the earth was once cursed for our sins, so it will also sometime be blessed and glorified because of our righteousness. The Angel Moroni said to the Prophet Joseph Smith that "the hearts of the children shall turn to their fathers. If it were not so, the whole earth would be utterly wasted at his coming." (Joseph Smith 2:39.) If the earth is to reach its divine destiny, we ourselves must participate in those upward changes.

Sometime ago, a welfare worker was telling me about living on a farm with his wife and five sons. When these sons became old enough, they were given a little of the family land to till and were allowed to have some of the family farm animals to raise. And, of course, when they did the work of the farm, they received the natural compensations that came as a consequence. The Lord has a program that is almost identical to this: when we are old enough and responsible enough, he invites us into his "family firm" and allows us to have a part in that great enterprise that Jesus referred to as "my Father's business." That is the business of building character, spirituality, and eternal life into the lives of his children.

When God finished his work of creation, the earth was a paradise, a great Garden of Eden that brought forth all good things abundantly. There was no sin upon the earth. The tree of the knowledge of good and evil was growing here, as was also the tree of life. But when disobedience was introduced, it brought its resulting mortality into the world, according to the foreknowledge and preordained plan of God. God announced this downward change when he said, ". . . cursed is the ground for thy sake. . . ." (Genesis 3:17.) In this telestial condition, the earth forms a suitable background for the weaknesses, tears, and suffering of our mortality.

2

The Son of God subsequently came to earth as the Redeemer of the earth. In pointing forward to one of the greatest objectives ever given, he prayed for our exaltation when, in his petition to God, he said, "Thy kingdom come. Thy will be done in earth, as it is in heaven." (Matthew 6:10.) But only we, with his help, can bring this heavenly condition about.

At the glorious second coming of Christ, the earth will be cleansed of its wickedness. Sin and weaknesses as we know them will be done away with, and they who remain will be they who obey God and keep his commandments. After the cleansing of the earth, the millennium of a thousand years of peace, accomplishment, and happiness will begin. The work of the earth will be completed by the godly people who will live upon it, and the earth will be renewed and its paradisiacal glory restored, as it becomes a paradise as it was in Garden of Eden days.

The story is told of a man who once took a friend to lunch. In the course of their conversation, one of the men proposed a problem to be solved by the other. He said, "Suppose your job was to get on the other side of the mountain. However, the mountain was so high that you could not go over it. It was so deep in the earth that you could not go under it. It was so long that you could not go around it. It was so thick that you could not go through it. How then would you get on the other side of the mountain?" His friend thought that it would be impossible. But the answer is simple. If one makes himself bigger than the mountain, the job is easy. No obstacle is an obstacle at all when it is smaller than we are, and we can become celestial people by making ourselves bigger than any evil thing that can happen to us.

When the work of this earth will have been finished, then will come the final judgment of all those who have ever lived upon the earth. Those who qualify for the celestial kingdom will be permitted to live here eternally, and this condition of complete righteousness will make it possible for the earth to again have its status increased so that it will become celestialized.

3

Then the object of the Master's prayer will be realized, and his will will be done upon the earth as it is now done in heaven. Then this will also be the heaven of those who have qualified as celestial beings. When that happens, each individual qualified to live here will have achieved the ultimate in his own success and happiness.

To help us qualify for our ultimate blessings in the celestial kingdom is the purpose for which the Church was organized, and every ordinance of the gospel has to do with the celestial kingdom. If we are not interested in the celestial kingdom, it is not necessary for us to be baptized. It is not necessary for us to be married in the temple, for those who belong to the lower kingdoms will not have their families anyway. If we are only interested in the lower kingdoms, it will not be necessary for us to pay our tithing or keep the Sabbath day holy. In the gospel of Jesus Christ, the Lord has given us no commandments to prepare us for the lower kingdoms. We qualify for the lower kingdoms by the degree of our default from the celestial.

However, if we are to live on a celestial earth, we must be celestial persons who have resurrected celestial bodies, who have celestial minds, celestial personalities, and celestial families, and who live by celestial laws. All of these were ordained for the specific benefit of those who would become celestial beings. The celestial is the order of life to which God himself belongs and for which he would like all of his children to qualify.

Those who have made of their homes a heaven and who have been valiant in the testimony of Jesus and have become bigger than the telestial or the terrestrial kingdoms will be exalted to celestial rank. The greatest good fortune of our lives is that we are the children of God and that we have been given the direction and the freedom to work unceasingly to promote the best interests of the family of God. It is hoped that the chapters of this book will help each of us understand better how we may proceed toward achieving this goal.

2
Identifying the Kingdom

One of the provocative happenings of our world took place nearly two thousand years ago when the wise men came out of the East and followed the star to the manger in Bethlehem. When they arrived in Jerusalem they sought direction for their course, saying, "Where is he who is born King of the Jews? for we have seen his star in the east, and are come to worship him." (Matthew 2:2.) And that is what wise men have been doing ever since that time.

The very core and center of our lives has to do with finding the King and then being constructive members of the kingdom. The journey of the wise men was over when they had found the King, and so is ours. The greatest tragedy of the lives of many is that they never find the King. Many of those who lived in the merdian of time met Jesus in the temple. They listened to his logic; they heard his testimony; they knew of his miracles. They knew that he had organized his church upon the foundation of apostles and prophets, with himself as the chief cornerstone. Yet they never accepted his doctrines or joined the church that he had organized for their eternal exaltation.

This problem of aloofness from God and failure to recognize his church is still a very serious problem to the churches of men that were organized by men and bear the names of men and teach precepts many of which are the doctrines of men. Many rationalize, saying that it doesn't matter which church a person belongs to or what he believes as long as he is sincere. Some cling to a man-made organization, saying, "I've belonged to this church too long to make a change now."

This willingness to follow men instead of God has always been one of the world's most serious problems. Isaiah recognized this fact when he said, "The earth also is defiled under the inhabitants thereof; because they have transgressed the laws, changed the ordinance, broken the ever-

5

lasting covenant. Therefore hath the curse devoured the earth, and they that dwell therein are desolate. . . ." (Isaiah 24:5-6.)

The scriptures make perfectly clear that there could not be more than one authorized church. The apostle Paul said, "There is . . . one Lord, one faith, one baptism, one God and Father of all. . . ." (Ephesians 4:4-6.)

He also indicated the seriousness of anyone presuming to set himself up to teach in the name of the Lord without authority to do so. To the Galatians Paul said, "But though we, or an angel from heaven, preach any other gospel unto you than that which we have preached unto you, let him be accursed." (Galatians 1:8.)

Men are all vulnerable so far as making mistakes is concerned, and it is very serious for anyone to select himself to minister in the affairs of Christ's church. The Savior himself said, "Ye have not chosen me, but I have chosen you. . . ." (John 15:16.) Paul said, "And no man taketh this honour unto himself, but he that is called of God, as was Aaron." (Hebrews 5:4.) This is one of the most widely violated commandments of the holy scriptures, for many men call themselves to the ministry and teach for doctrine their own ideas.

The great Protestant reformers, and many men since that time, knowing that the original church organized by Christ had been corrupted by apostasy and changes made in doctrines, took it upon themselves to try to reform the theology of the church and, in the process, without divine authority or direction, organized churches of their own, called them by their own names, and taught their own doctrines. These reformers were themselves frequently in error, for two conflicting statements cannot both be correct. As a result of the work of the protesters, the Christian world had many man-made churches. They did more to introduce confusion into the minds of people than they did to purify the apostasy that they recognized in the mother church. Because teaching false doctrine is such a serious sin, it naturally follows that to identify with such a group makes one an accessory to evil. The Lord condemned this very fault as he found it being practiced in his own day by

6

splinter groups known as the pharisees, sadducees, essenes, and the other conflicting groups. He said to them, ". . . ye shut up the kingdom of heaven against men: for ye neither go in yourselves, neither suffer ye them that are entering to go in." (Matthew 23:13.)

Many people in these unauthorized Christian churches frankly and honestly admit that their church has no authority or power to minister the ordinances of the gospel, and yet by their influence they draw other people into the same error.

Christ himself indicated that he alone was the door to the sheepfold, that there were certain specified qualifications and procedures for entrance, and that anyone who tried to come in by any other way was a thief and a robber. (See John 10:7-8.) This conforms to the important precept of Jesus that "strait is the gate and narrow is the way, which leadeth unto life, and few there be that find it." (Matthew 7:14.)

This practice of teaching one's own beliefs is one of the doctrines of men that Jesus was so vigorous in denouncing. In the book of Revelation we read these words: "For I testify unto every man that heareth the words of the prophecy of this book, If any man shall add unto these things, God shall add unto him the plagues that are written in this book: And if any man shall take away from the words of the book of this prophecy, God shall take away his part out of the book of life, and out of the holy city, and from the things which are written in this book." (Revelation 22:18-19.)

If everyone who chooses to do so has a divine right to organize his own church and teach his own doctrines under the pretext of reforming the original churches, then everyone else also has a right to organize his own church under the pretext of reforming the protesting churches. This can conceivably lead to everybody having his own organization, no matter how far it may be away from the truth and righteousness. This doctrine is seriously condemned in the scriptures, for it leads to endless confusion and error. This is that sin warned against by the Savior, wherein the blind lead the blind and they all fall together. This error of men

7

taking unto themselves the divine authority for reforming somebody else is what led to the crucifixion of Jesus and imposed violent death upon all but one of the divinely appointed apostles. This procedure is still one of the most serious of all sins, because men have transgressed the laws, changed the ordinances, and broken the everlasting covenant. In fulfillment of the prophecy of Isaiah, a great apostasy from God has taken place.

There are at least four ways in which one may identify the Church of Jesus Christ as the only true and living church upon the face of the earth.

1. The blueprint. The blueprint that the Lord himself gave for his church is plainly described in the New Testament. The true church must have the same organization and the same authority, and it must teach the same doctrines and practice the same ordinances.

2. A personal testimony. The Lord has provided that everyone may have a personal testimony for himself. Jesus said, "Ask, and it shall be given you; seek, and ye shall find; knock, and it shall be opened unto you." (Matthew 7:7.)

3. Live the commandments. Jesus said, "If any man will do his [the Father's] will, he shall know of the doctrine. . . ." (John 7:17.) Many people say, "If I knew that God was alive and the Church was true, I would live the gospel principles." These people are turned around backwards. God has not promised that he will reveal his will to criminals, atheists, and sinners. He has said that he will reveal his will to those who keep his commandments. Everyone may know for a cerainty that the principles of the gospel are true if he lives them.

4. Our own reason. God has equipped each of us with a magnificent piece of equipment called a brain, which is endowed with the power of reason. I was not present at Mount Sinai when the Ten Commandments were given, and yet I know just as surely as those who were there knew that it is wrong to steal and kill and be immoral. I know that those who keep the Sabbath day holy will be a different kind of people than those who do not. Reason tells me that the one who begat the Lord Jesus Christ is not some in-

comprehensible, shapeless, sexless mass that fills the universe. It tells me that God, the Eternal Heavenly Father, is in form and feature that great being in whose image man was created. My intellect, inspired by the light perceived from God, tells me that good is good and evil is evil.

As predicted in the scriptures, the Church of Jesus Christ has been restored to the earth in these latter days. The blueprint that was given 1900 years ago by the Lord himself is being strictly followed by the true church because it is the truth, the whole truth, and nothing but the truth. And if we follow the principles of the gospel in every detail, we can avoid the serious confusion that is presently troubling so many people.

The Lord has given us three great volumes of new scripture outlining in every detail the simple doctrines of the gospel that have been taught upon the earth since time began. These doctrines were outlined by the Savior of the world himself in his own dispensation, so that no one needs leave that strait and narrow way except by his own choice. May God help us to find the King and to be loyal members of his kingdom.

3
Flesh and Bones

Our earth is made up of some very interesting elements, including hydrogen, oxygen, nitrogen, carbon, magnesium, copper, zinc, silver, gold, platinum, and iron. In addition we can get all sorts of additional things by an almost unlimited number of combinations of the elements.

Among the most interesting substances found on our earth are those of which we ourselves are composed. In the beginning God selected out of the dust of the ground those elements from which he made up our wonderful bodies of flesh and bones. He not only fashioned us in his own image, but he also endowed us with the primal, godly element called *life*. He included in us a miraculous power that no one understands, called *procreation,* through which we may also form children in our own image.

Our flesh and bones are much more exciting to live with than if we have been made of ivory, platinum, radium, or diamonds. Even the Son of God, who spent a long term ruling with his Father in heaven, came to our earth at least in part to acquire a body of flesh and bones comparable to our own. Of this important event the scripture says:

"In the beginning was the Word, and the Word was with God, and the Word was God.

"The same was in the beginning with God.

"All things were made by him; and without him was not anything made that was made.

"In him was life; and the life was the light of men. . . .

"And the Word was made flesh, and dwelt among us, (and we beheld his glory, the glory as of the begotten of the Father,) full of grace and truth." (John 1:1-4, 14.)

Before his mortal birth, Jesus had a powerful body of spirit just as we were. Spirit is a much finer substance than flesh, although it is just as tangible and material as our mortal bodies. In this life, no one has ever seen his own spirit. However, in a modern-day revelation, the Lord has said, "There is no such thing as immaterial matter. All spirit is matter, but it is more fine or pure, and can only be discerned by purer eyes." (D&C 131:7.)

Before his mortal birth, Jesus had a powerful body of spirit. Some two thousand years before Bethlehem, he appeared to a prophet of great faith, the brother of Jared. He also revealed that at a later date he would come to the earth to take upon himself a mortal body. He permitted the brother of Jared to see his spiritual body and said, "Behold, this body, which ye now behold, is the body of my spirit; and man have I created after the body of my spirit; and even as I appear unto thee to be in the spirit will I appear unto my people in the flesh." (Ether 3:16.)

Concerning our progression through the three important parts of our eternal lives, the prophet Abraham said, "And they who keep their first estate shall be added upon; and they who keep not their first estate shall not have glory in the same kingdom with those who keep their first estate; and they who keep their second estate shall have glory added upon their heads for ever and ever." (Abraham 3:26.)

Next to our immortal spirits, this body of flesh and bones is undoubtedly the most valuable and most fantastic possession that any of us will ever have. The scriptures say that without it we could never have a fulness of joy.

A body includes a miraculous brain able to contain more information than a whole library of books. A prominent British neurophysicist recently said that no one could construct an electronic computer for three billion dollars that would be the equivalent of a human brain. Even so, who could endow an electronic computer with wisdom, judgment, reason, kindness, or logic, or who could give it the miraculous powers of human personality? Who could install into a computer the emotions of love, patriotism, loyalty, godliness, and happiness? Or who could invent a computer equipped with those fantastic and delightful human senses of sight, sound, taste, smell, touch, and imagination?

Now try to imagine what the glories of our flesh will be after it has been resurrected, celestialized, and glorified. At birth, Jesus was temporarily added upon with flesh and bones. But in the resurrection after his death, his spirit and body were inseparably joined together, never again to be separated. Our refined, resurrected bodies will be given many exciting characteristics that they do not now possess. In the resurrection the total body of flesh and spirit will be given great power, and it will no longer be subject to the laws of this mortal earth. In trying to help us to understand this great human creation, one scripture says, "What is man, that thou art mindful of him? and the son of man, that thou visitest him? For thou hast made him a little lower than the angels, and hast crowned him with glory and honour." (Psalm 8:4-5.)

For some thirty-three years Jesus was also made temporarily lower than he had been while he was creating worlds. Then after his forty-day post-resurrection ministry, he met his apostles on the Mount of Olives and gave them his final earthly instruction. The record says:

"And when he had spoken these things, while they beheld, he was taken up; and a cloud received him out of their sight.

"And while they looked stedfastly toward heaven as he went up, behold, two men stood by them in white apparel;

"Which also said, Ye men of Galilee, why stand ye gazing up into heaven? this same Jesus, which is taken up from you into heaven, shall so come in like manner as ye have seen him go into heaven." (Acts 1:9-11.)

After the resurrection Jesus was not restrained by the laws of gravity as he had hitherto been, nor were his movements hindered by any material obstructions. The scripture says, "And after eight days again his disciples were within, and Thomas with them: then came Jesus, the doors being shut, and stood in the midst, and said, Peace be unto you." (John 20:26.)

"But they were terrified and affrighted, and supposed that they had seen a spirit.

"And he said unto them, Why are ye troubled? and why do thoughts arise in your hearts?

"Behold my hands and my feet, that it is I myself: handle me, and see; for a spirit hath not flesh and bones, as ye see me have.

"And when he had thus spoken, he shewed them his hands and his feet.

"And while they yet believed not for joy, and wondered, he said unto them, Have ye here any meat?

"And they gave him a piece of broiled fish, and of an honeycomb.

"And he took it, and did eat before them." (Luke 24:37-43.)

What a tremendous fact that God, spirits, angels, and men all belong to the same species! They are only in different stages of development and in different degrees of righteousness. The offspring of celestial, resurrected beings are spirits, and after they have properly learned the lessons of their first estate and have adequately proven themselves as spirits, they are added upon with wonderful, beautiful bodies of flesh and bones. When we successfully pass the requirements of our second estate, then glory shall be added upon our heads forever and ever.

In the resurrection, our bodies themselves are made immortal. Even now our bodies of flesh and bones have tremendous significance, and we can only imagine how that importance will be magnified for the future. Someone has said:

> If God has made this world so fair,
> Where sin and death abound,
> How beautiful beyond compare
> Will paradise be found.

If bodies of flesh and bones were not important, they never would have been created in the first place. If they were not necessary for eternity, then the resurrection would never have been instituted. If a body of flesh and bones were not necessary for God the Father, then God the Son would never have been resurrected.

13

Sometime ago, I saw and heard a lecture given by a sculptor to a group of salesmen. In clay, he was fashioning before them his conception of a salesman. He was putting in all of the parts that, in his opinion, a good salesman needed. He explained that every human being has 206 bones. They provide the framework that gives the body its strength and form. As the sculptor worked, he talked to the salesmen about the importance of that bony structure that houses the equipment for the center of intelligence called the brain. Therefore, he gave the symbolic clay salesman a broad forehead to represent his thinking ability.

With an attempt at some humor, the sculptor pointed out some of the other bones that also have some symbolic importance. Every person has two cheekbones, and Jesus indicated that when one is smitten on one cheek, he should turn the other. One is very fortunate who has a good jawbone, for occasionally he needs to "take it on the chin."

Certainly every person ought to have a good backbone, for there are many heavy loads that each must carry. The backbone connects the head and thorax with the abdomen, from which the legs are operated. It supports the rib cage, which houses the body's vital internal organs. It also encases that great cable of nerves called the spinal cord. The backbone itself is made up of twenty-five individual bony sections called vertebrae. Each one has outlets for that vast number of nerves that serve and control the rest of the body.

Everyone should also have a vigorous wishbone. Symbolically this is the center of his hopes, dreams, and ambitions. This is the place where plans are made and put into operation. The whole being is greatly enriched when one has a prominent funnybone operating a good sense of humor to keep the personality well lubricated.

This great combination of flesh, feeling, intelligence, vision, and emotions supported by these 206 useful bones is endowed with the primal, godly element of life and accounts for man, God's greatest creation. There are different kinds of life in the universe, varying from a weed to a tree, and from a worm to a man.

How grateful we ought to be that we are not made of stone or steel or wood! How grateful we should feel that we can look forward to a much more exciting metamorphosis than that which makes a caterpillar into a beautiful butterfly! I would not like to be a rock sitting on the mountainside for a thousand years without any thought or feelings of emotion, and I am grateful that I am not one of those eternal spirits who, by their disobedience, lost the right to be added upon with God's glorious creation of flesh and bones.

I love the present possibilities of life, but how thrilled I am that I was begotten of God! How grateful I am that in heaven God ordained both male and female! God established the family as the basic unit of life to last throughout eternity. How proud I am and ought to be of my eternal heavenly parents and of my eternal brothers and sisters!

How grateful I am that I am a child of God, possessing all of the wonderful possibilities of thought and love, and with a personality destined to become like God, who has ordained glory and happiness to be the eternal purposes of life!

4
Meet the Mormons

In 1965 a book prepared by Doyle L. Green and Randall L. Green was published by Deseret Book Company. This book gives a great deal of information about the history of the Church as established in the days of Jesus. It also discusses briefly the great apostasy following the ministry of Jesus and the restoration of the gospel in the latter days. It enumerates some of the significant doctrines taught in both dispensations and gives some of the accomplishments of the Church in the latter days. The title of this book is *Meet the Mormons.*

In 1973 a moving picture was made at Brigham Young University on this same subject and under the same title. It shows scenes taken from around the world of the activities and beliefs of those who are members of this rapidly growing church.

Thomas Carlyle gave us something to think about when he said that a man's religion is the most important thing about him. That is what he thinks about, believes in, works at, fights for, and lives by. The primary purpose of the ministry of Christ was to help the people of the earth live those great doctrines of salvation which would help to bring about the eternal exaltation of their own souls. His teachings were met with vigorous opposition, though they contained the most important ideas in the world. The people did not accept the Savior himself, and though they were exposed to many wonderful principles, they passed them off by saying such things as "Is not this the carpenter's son? . . ." (Matthew 13:55), and "Can any good come out of Nazareth?" (John 1:46).

After Christ's ministry of some three years, his life itself was taken, and in time all of his chosen twelve met violent deaths except John the Revelator, who was banished to that little island of Patmos in the Aegean Sea. As a consequence of the lack of discernment and faith in the lives of the people to whom Jesus ministered, dark ages fell upon the world and the people themselves lost those godly blessings that could have been theirs merely by a little investigation and study. The fact that the authorized prophets of God have always had such a difficult time in getting their message accepted should caution us and help us to avoid the mistake of ourselves rejecting the Lord's message, as so many others have done.

Anyone who is familiar with and believes in the Bible cannot help but understand that we are now living in the greatest of all dispensations. This is the one that the apostle Paul referred to as the dispensation of the fulness of times when all things should be brought together in one. (See Ephesians 1:10.) Peter also referred to our day as the restitution of all things spoken by all the holy prophets since the world began. (See Acts 3:21.) Therefore, it is inconceivable under these circumstances that we should not expect some direct revelation from God in this greatest of all ages.

It is also evident that if we can read the signs of the times, we may know that the glorious second coming of Christ is very near at hand. And amid the wars and rumors of wars that should immediately precede his second coming, Jesus pointed out a bright spot in our latter days when he said that "this gospel of the kingdom should be preached in all the world for a witness to all nations; and then shall the end come." (Matthew 24:14.)

The people of the earth failed to accept the gospel message in the days of Jesus himself, and this second chance will not last for very long before the great winding-up scene takes place. The Savior himself said, "Now learn a parable of the fig tree; When his branch is yet tender, and putteth forth leaves, ye know that summer is nigh: So likewise ye, when ye shall see all these things, know that it is near, even at the doors." (Matthew 24:32-33.)

It must seem strange to many people that The Church of Jesus Christ of Latter-day Saints should claim that there has been a divine restoration of the gospel by holy beings in our day, and yet the Bible clearly states that such a restoration must be made before the end comes. And that is exactly what is claimed by the Latter-day Saints. An enthusiastic invitation is extended to every person upon the earth to "meet the Mormons" and investigate the tremendous claims being made by them.

The important facts claimed for the restoration are fully supported by the scriptures. This may seem particularly difficult to some because this is a day when so many people say that miracles have ceased and that God no longer reveals himself by direct communication to his people upon the earth. But why should God remain silent about religion when so many important developments are taking place in every other field?

Sometime ago a press dispatch indicated that of all the scientists who have ever lived upon the earth, 80 percent of them are alive now. Of course, no one could deny that we live in the greatest age of wonders and miracles that has ever been known upon our planet. And if God would reserve his greatest inventors and scientists and businessmen to come forth in our day, it might seem very strange to think that he would neglect the most important aspect of his work, which has always been religion and the personal salvation of his children.

Of course the word *Mormon* is not the actual name of the Church. Just as the members of Christ's church were nicknamed Christians in the meridian dispensation, so the members of The Church of Jesus Christ of Latter-day Saints have been nicknamed in these latter days after a great pre-Columbus American prophet by the name of Mormon. Because Christ knew that the great culture that existed in the western hemisphere before Columbus would be destroyed, he called Mormon at a very early age to accumulate some of his people's important scriptures and compile them into a book so that we who would come after their civilization had been destroyed might have their teachings and records. These compiled writings are called the Book of Mormon, and they contain a fulness of the gospel to the people on the western hemisphere, just as the Bible is the record of God's dealings with his people in the eastern hemisphere.

If one is properly introduced to the Mormons, he is introduced to the pre-Columbus American scriptures written by prophets of God who lived in the western hemisphere from approximately 2000 B.C. until their civilization destroyed itself nearly four hundred years after Christ had personally ministered among them following his crucifixion and resurrection in Jerusalem. These events are easy to believe if they are understood, and several million people around the earth bear fervent testimony that they are true. As the Latter-day Saints, or Mormons, testify, all of the doctrines of original Christianity have been restored to the earth. There has also been a restoration of Christ's own authority to minister in all of the important doctrines of salvation. The Prophet Joseph Smith was once asked how he governed such a divergent group of people, who had different backgrounds, different languages, and different cultures, and were gathered from all around the world. His reply was, "I teach them correct principles, and they govern themselves."

Dr. Henry C. Link once said that nothing puts so much order into human life as to live by a set of sound principles. The most sound principles in the world are the principles of the gospel.

During the apostasy and the dark ages that followed, some of the precious gospel truths were lost, and thus the original church of Christ was splintered into hundreds of contending sects, all containing some good and yet seriously differing in their understanding of many of the important doctrines of Christ. In our day God has given us three great volumes of new scripture outlining in every detail the simple principles of the gospel of Christ, teachings that completely support and make clear his original teachings. These books are the Book of Mormon, the Doctrine and Covenants, and the Pearl of Great Price.

The Book of Mormon itself says that it would come forth in a day when people were doubting and denying the Bible. The purpose of the Book of Mormon is to help to persuade *all* people that Jesus is the Christ, the Eternal Son of God. That should be worth thoughtful investigation, for there are millions of people throughout the world who bear testimony that the gospel of Jesus Christ has been again restored to the earth.

If these great principles were fully understood, believed in, and lived by everyone, this earth would soon be God's paradise. The restored gospel makes powerful restatement of the value of the atonement of Christ, of the truths of the literal bodily resurrection, of the three degrees of glory, and of the possibilities of eternal progression.

On February 27, 1833, a revelation was given called the Word of Wisdom, indicating the destructiveness of liquor, tobacco, and other harmful substances. The Lord has given some modern revelations about the marriage covenant and the eternal nature of the family organization and has directed that temples should be built around the world where these sacred covenants can be properly performed.

A great deal of new information has been given concerning salvation for the dead. It has also been restated that the glorious second coming of Christ is near at hand. We are now living in the greatest and final of all of the dispensations of time. Many of the ancient prophets looked down with envy to our time and some of them almost lived in our day. From his lonely isolation on Patmos, John the Revelator looked to our day and described what he saw:

"And I saw another angel fly in the midst of heaven, having the everlasting gospel to preach unto them that dwell on the earth, and to every nation, and kindred, and tongue, and people,

"Saying with a loud voice, Fear God, and give glory to him; for the hour of his judgment is come: and worship him that made heaven, and earth, and the sea, and the fountains of waters." (Revelation 14:6-7.)

What a great tragedy it is that we not only reject the new revelations of the Lord, but also that so many people have also laid aside the Bible itself! We have in many cases discontinued our belief in the Ten Commandments and the Sermon on the Mount. Many people are saying that God is dead or has lost interest in our welfare, or that he has no power or desire to reveal himself in this time of our most critical need.

What a challenge for everyone in the world to meet the Mormons and to instigate an investigation that could be the most profitable experience in their lives and help to bring about the eternal exaltation of their souls! May God bless everyone to make the most of this important and friendly invitation.

5
The Church Hath Need of Every Member

As one of his greatest literary masterpieces, the apostle Paul wrote his famous twelfth chapter of First Corinthians. He pointed to the human body as an example of completeness. The body has many members, each of which serves a different function and each of which is necessary. However, there is only one body.

"And the eye cannot say to the hand, I have no need of thee: nor again the head to the feet, I have no need of you." (1 Corinthians 12:21.)

There are a great many meanings attached to this idea. We have many different spiritual gifts that are all from the same spirit. Paul referred to the many different officers that the Lord placed in the church and said:

"And God hath set some in the church, first apostles, secondarily prophets, thirdly teachers, after that miracles, then gifts of healings, helps, governments, diversities of tongues.

"Are all apostles? are all prophets? are all teachers? are all workers of miracles?

"Have all the gifts of healing? do all speak with tongues? do all interpret?" (1 Corinthians 12:28-30.)

Paul also said, "Now ye are the body of Christ, and members in particular." (1 Corinthians 12:27.)

"And those members of the body, which we think to be less honourable, upon these we bestow more abundant honour; and our uncomely parts have more abundant comeliness.

"For our comely parts have no need: but God hath tempered the body together, having given more abundant honour to that part which lacked:

"That there should be no schism in the body; but that the members should have the same care one for another.

"And whether one member suffer, all the members suffer with it; or one member be honoured, all the members rejoice with it." (1 Corinthians 12:23-26.)

Christ organized his church, and it is important that every one of his children should belong to it so that each can be uplifted and edified by the others. God loves every one of his children, and there is great joy in his heart when any one of us does well, and he feels great sorrow when one soul strays away or is lost.

God's love for his children is far greater than that of any earthly parent. However, God's children are exposed to many serious hazards. The Lord said to Peter: "Simon, Simon, behold, Satan hath desired to have you, that he may sift you as wheat." (Luke 22:31.) Satan wants *all* of God's children, and because of disobedience, some of God's most-loved offspring may have to go and live forever with Satan amid the awful torments, failures, and unhappiness of an unpleasant, everlasting hell. Because God does not want to let any of his children go, he has tried to prevent it from happening by organizing his children into families and establishing his church upon the earth. He has given to parents and to his inspired church leaders a command, saying, ". . . Feed my sheep." (John 21:17.)

In placing his value upon the human soul, God has compared it to wealth of the entire earth. He has also offered great rewards to anyone who will help any of his children to successfully pass the requirements of their mortal estate so that they can live eternally with God. The Master said:

"And if it so be that you should labor all your days in crying repentance unto this people, and bring, save it be one soul unto me, how great shall be your joy with him in the kingdom of my Father!

"And now, if your joy will be great with one soul that you have brought unto me into the kingdom of my Father,

23

how great will be your joy if you should bring many souls unto me!" (D&C 18:15-16.)

If our reward will be so great because of one soul that has been brought unto him, what will our regret be if, by our negligence or bad example, one soul or many souls shall be lost? Suppose that because we do not magnify our callings as parents, friends, or church leaders, some of God's children fail to reach their designed destination. God is the God of love, our eternal Heavenly Father. He hates evil, but he loves his children with an intensity beyond our understanding. Each of us has been given our freedom, and if we do not use it in the right way, great benefits will be lost.

God has made an unchangeable, everlasting commitment to the free agency of every one of his children. To help us, he has given us intelligence, reason, a conscience, the promptings of the still small voice, and a full set of the holy scriptures. He wants every one of us to be saved in the highest degree of glory. He has already paid a fantastic amount for our exaltation and has made it clear that our success is tremendously important to him. He has said:

"Remember the worth of souls is great in the sight of God;

"For, behold, the Lord your Redeemer suffered death in the flesh; wherefore he suffered the pain of all men, that all men might repent and come unto him.

"And he hath risen again from the dead, that he might bring all men unto him, on conditions of repentance.

"And how great is his joy in the soul that repenteth!" (D&C 18:10-13.)

"And also all they who receive this priesthood receive me, saith the Lord;

"For he that receiveth my servants receiveth me;

"And he that receiveth me receiveth my Father;

"And he that receiveth my Father receiveth my Father's kingdom; therefore all that my Father hath shall be given unto him.

"And this is according to the oath and covenant which belongeth to the priesthood.

"Therefore, all those who receive this priesthood, receive this oath and covenant of my Father, which he cannot break, neither can it be moved.

"But whoso breaketh this covenant after he hath received it, and altogether turneth therefrom, shall not have forgiveness of sins in this world nor in the world to come." (D&C 84:35-41.)

If anyone is lost, then everyone is the loser, because, as pointed out by Paul, we are all a part of the same body, and one cannot say to another, "I have no need of thee." We are all members of the family of God, and no family can be perfect without all of its members.

On one occasion the Lord said:

"Behold, I will send you Elijah the prophet before the coming of the great and dreadful day of the Lord:

"And he shall turn the heart of the fathers to the children, and the heart of the children to their fathers, lest I come and smite the earth with a curse." (Malachi 4:5-6.)

We have an important interest in every other man's deeds. When one person beautifies the landscape or discovers a health formula or invents some labor-saving device, then the whole community is enriched. When the tide comes in, all of the ships in the harbor are lifted up. When one man improves the frontiers of his own mind or spirit, the spiritual and intellectual level of the entire world is raised.

When anyone's salvation is wasted we are also the losers. When one of God's children is eternally lost, a part of us is lost also.

One of the great experiences of my life took place many years ago when I served as bishop and could go to my own ward every Sunday. I was always greatly stimulated by those who attended. We had in our ward a member of the Sunday School general board. Because of his other assignments, he could only attend our ward occasionally, but I remember how my pleasure used to soar when he was present.

With him in the audience, our ward seemed much more like a going concern.

One of my heroines of that day was a seventy-five-year-old widow. When she was a young woman her husband had died, leaving her to support their children by doing the heavy work on the farm. I knew much of her background, and what a thrill it always gave me to shake her hand, express my love for her, and feel her courage, faith, and friendly response. And every other person in the ward was also important to me personally for varied reasons.

It is still true that down the broad way of life no one walks alone; each stands at the head of some kind of caravan. When Satan rebelled against God and walked out of heaven, one-third of all of the hosts of heaven walked out right behind him. If he had repented and come back, others would also have returned. And if the most inactive, spiritually backward member of the ward comes to church, he makes things happier for someone else and raises the general level for everyone. In the same way, when some fall down, everyone loses.

Everyone in the world has some abilities and personality traits given for the perfection of the whole. And to be complete, the church needs every member and every non-member. May God help us to be complete and to help the Church, the world, and the Lord to be complete also.

6
Inventory

An important part of any business is its inventory. A businessman is placed at a serious disadvantage if he doesn't know how much merchandise he has on his shelves and what its value is. The dictionary says that an inventory is a detailed list of articles that gives for each the code number, description, and value. An inventory is a kind of catalog, a formal list of the various items of property belonging to a particular person or firm.

An inventory may also be a tally of one's individual personality traits, aptitudes, attitudes, and skills. Such a personal inventory may be used for the purpose of planning one's own life or analyzing or counseling himself.

The scriptures mention many of the items that we should incorporate into our personal inventory on a permanent basis. For example, we read:

"Whatever principle of intelligence we attain unto in this life, it will rise with us in the resurrection.

"And if a person gains more knowledge and intelligence in this life through his diligence and obedience than another, he will have so much the advantage in the world to come." (D&C 130:18-19.)

Other scriptures make it perfectly clear that now is the time to build up an inventory for our eternal lives.

Our inventory supplies a kind of capital on which our various incomes of joys, peace, and prosperity are calculated. There are some other items that we might also include in our personal capital. Over the years I have gone through an interesting process of making up a kind of literary inventory. Some of the headings are as follows:

1. *My Ideas*

Victor Hugo once said that there is nothing in the world as powerful as an idea whose time has come. And an idea's time comes when we get a harness on it so that it can work for us.

Abraham Lincoln once said, "What I want to know is in books, and my best friend is the one who will get me a book that I haven't read." What wonderful treasures we have in the holy scriptures, the great biographies, histories, books of science, books of inspiration, and even fiction.

Many years ago, near the end of World War II, I heard an exciting lecture given by Dr. Adam S. Bennion on the values in great literature. He said: "Suppose that you were going to be a prisoner in a prisoner of war camp for the next four years and that you could take with you the works of any ten authors. Which would you take, and what would you expect to get out of them?"

It is fairly easy to sell the idea of great literature to most people. However, they destroy the idea and miss the benefits by saying, "I am too busy," or "I don't have time to read." It is interesting that we do have time to read about the world's crime and violence in the newspapers. We do have time to watch television and go to the movies, but usually we don't have time for the greatest human thought. And most of us excuse ourselves from doing the things that we know that we ought to do by being too busy doing those things that we know we should not do.

Dr. Bennion suggested that one should select the ten authors whose lives he would like most to emulate, and, in turn, read every word they had ever written. That is a great idea, and finally I generated enough courage to make a start.

At that time I was teaching a class in salesmanship, and I reread the Bible with the idea of getting out of it its salesmanship ideas. The Bible is the world's first book of religion. It is the world's first book of history. It is the world's first book of literature. It is also the world's first book of salesmanship. If I were trying to teach someone to be a good salesman, I would encourage him to absorb the faith, the convictions, the courage, the enthusiasm, and the righteousness found in the Bible. The best way for anyone to be a good salesman is to first be a good man. He ought to try to get the spirit of the young man from Nazareth who went around saying to people such things as, "Be of good cheer. Be not afraid. Why are ye troubled? Why do thoughts arise in your hearts? Rejoice, and be exceeding glad." Jesus said to people, "Be ye doers of the word. Be ye therefore perfect. Think no evil. Enter ye in at the strait gate. Be ye clean that bear the vessels of the Lord." All of this is good salesmanship.

Every time one reads the Bible with a new purpose, it becomes a new book. When we read the Bible for its salesmanship, it is quite a different book than when we read it for its theology or its literature. And I had a tremendous new experience with the Bible. This gave me enough heart to take up Shakespeare. I suppose that Shakespeare comes close to the top of most people's list of great authors. Understanding Shakespeare was a little difficult for me at first. I had to reread a lot and to look up many meanings that I didn't understand. But finally the clouds began to open up a little and a new light of understanding started to break through, and I had an exciting and wonderful experience as I put some harnesses on Shakespeare.

Then, in turn, I read the complete works of Emerson, twenty-eight volumes of Elbert Hubbard, and fourteen volumes of 19,000 pages of the eloquent but atheistic Robert G. Ingersoll. I read the fifty volumes of the Harvard classics and eighteen volumes of Harry Emerson Fosdick. And in the last quarter of a century I have read a total of 983 volumes of some of the world's greatest books. I have become much more intimately acquainted with Homer, Milton, Dante, Saul of Tarsus, and Jesus of Nazareth. I read as carefully and as thoughtfully as I can, and always with a pencil in my hand.

I think of my reading in terms of the combine harvester out on the farm. It sweeps across a field of wheat and cuts everything, but in the threshing process it throws out all of the weeds, the chaff, and the straw, and puts the clean wheat into the sack. I do a similar kind of mental threshing. I mark all the ideas I think will be helpful to me. I make some decisions about them and prepare myself to utilize them before I leave them. These especially selected ideas are then copied into my twenty-five notebooks, totaling some

7,500 pages of closely typed notes. Then I go back and memorize the most interesting and exciting of these ideas. The rest I stamp as deep as possible into my brain cells. I could probably recite a hundred pages of Shakespeare, and I have a speaking acquaintance with much more. With some memorization, it is much easier to retain the flavor, power, beauty, color, and meaning that this great master worked so hard to give to his ideas. People sometimes make notes on the backs of envelopes and then put them in drawers or files or pigeon holes. However, that is not the way to retain ideas—that is the popular way to lose ideas.

If I were going on a trip and wanted to take my most exciting reading material, I wouldn't take Shakespeare or Emerson or the Harvard Classics. I would take my notes. So far as I am concerned, there is no chaff or waste in them. There is only the good wheat or the pure gold that has been fully refined. Included are the workable ideas, the sound philosophies, the harmonious poems, the satisfying arguments, and the life-saving scriptures that I know the best and love the most. And these are the ones that I can use most advantageously. Out of my vast paper memory, I reap a large income of satisfactions and uplift.

2. My Heroes

In 1899 a large sum of money was given to New York University to build the Hall of Fame for Great Americans. I am grateful for those fine persons memorialized in the American Hall of Fame, which includes many of America's founding fathers and others who have helped to make America and Americans great. However, I have an even finer group of heroes in my own hall of fame, which I also carry around with me in my own mind and heart. My hall of fame is peopled with heroes of my own choosing. I have personally carved their portraits and literally written upon their tablets. Each of my tablets takes about sixteen minutes to read, and I can spend an hour in my mental hall of fame and run the greatness of my heroes through my own mind again and again. I am sure that Carl Sandburg loved Abraham Lincoln far more because he was Lincoln's biographer. And just as I can be thoroughly thrilled by the great music and the beautiful art with which I am most intimately familiar, so I can also be most readily inspired by the biographies that I myself have written and therefore understand and appreciate. To enjoy an interview with my heroes, I am never kept waiting in anterooms or outer offices. My heroes always have time to give me all of the attention I need, and our interviews are on the most intimate and friendly basis.

I have included in my hall of fame many of the great prophets, some of the captains of industry, some of the great athletes, writers, scholars, and leaders of nations. I have included Joan of Arc, Madame Curie, Winston Churchill, and Mahondas K. Gandhi; and in an especially favored place I have carved the portrait and written the tablet of my mother.

3. My Success Stories

Everyone is by instinct a natural collector. A child often starts his collecting career by gathering rocks, colored glass, string, chalk, and marbles. A little later he upgrades his inventory by collecting bank accounts, stocks and bonds, real estate, and life insurance policies. Some people collect stamps, some collect coins, some collect butterflies, some tapestries, and some pieces of great art.

Since 1966 I have been collecting success stories. A success story is a small section of the successful experience of someone else that may be extracted and made negotiable in my bloodstream. To this point in time I have written down and memorized seventy-two of the finest and most usable parts of success that I have discovered in others, and I am fitting them into my own mental, moral, and spiritual machinery.

4. My Gallery of Art

Pictures have always been very helpful. "One picture is worth a thousand words," someone has said. On March 17, 1941, President Franklin D. Roosevelt dedicated our National Gallery of Art in Washington, D.C. The building cost 16 million dollars and houses a collection of 126 paintings by the Old Masters and 26 pieces of sculpture that were valued at that time at approximately $80 million, or an average of over $500,000 each. The gallery and an endowment fund to maintain it were presented to the American people as a gift by the late Andrew W. Mellon.

I have some inspiring picture books containing pictures of my own, and in addition, I have a few $500,000 pictures painted on my mind and heart.

5. *My Word Pictures*

Probably the most inspiring pictures are not painted with paint on canvases. They are painted with words and emotions on human minds and souls. For my own inspiration I have painted some word pictures of such subjects as loyalty, integrity, dependability, faith, beauty, and devotion to God. Among the great pictures from the scriptures, I see Jesus dressed in shining garments standing on the top of the Mount of Transfiguration. I have many other pictures that enrich the courage, righteousness, and industry of my own life. My prayer is that God will help all of us build the inventories of our lives.

7

The Fruits of the Spirit

One of the reasons for the great excellence in the teachings of Jesus was his ability to draw meaningful comparisons. He was able to make difficult things clear by comparing them with those more simple things that could be readily understood. One of the most common of his comparisons came out of his horticultural background. He often compared the lives of people with the trees, vines, and seeds with which he was familiar. He was the sower of seeds, the grower of good plants, the one who pruned out the dead wood and the unproductive branches, that there might be a more abundant harvest.

This more abundant life was not so much about horticulture as it was about human-culture, and he made an application not only to our mortality but to our immortality as well. When anyone understands God's plan for our eternal exaltation, the one thing that he is usually impressed with is the lack of limitations placed on our progress except those that we ourselves impose. To bring about our own abundance Jesus said:

"Judge not, and ye shall not be judged: condemn not, and ye shall not be condemned: forgive, and ye shall be forgiven:

"Give, and it shall be given unto; good measure, pressed down, and shaken together, and running over, shall men give into your bosom. For with the same measure that ye mete withal it shall be measured to you again." (Luke 6:37-38.)

There is no sign of any limitation here. In his parables Jesus was not talking about how to increase the yields of the vines and the trees; he always measured his proposed abundance in terms of the productivity of human life. And yet think of the abundance of some of God's other creations.

Almost every one of God's plants produces enough seeds that if they were all replanted, the result would cover the earth in just a very short time. It has been estimated that 95 percent of all of the things required to produce a good crop of wheat has already been provided by creation in the soil, the air, the rainfall, the climate, and the sunshine. The other 5 percent consists in the planting and harvesting that is done by us.

It was one of the primary concerns of Jesus that none of his creations should be unproductive. We remember that on one occasion he searched a fig tree for fruit and when he found none, he cursed the tree so that it withered away and died. He made one of his most significant proclamations when he said, "Every tree that bringeth not forth good fruit is hewn down, and cast into the fire." (Matthew 7:19.)

In the days of Jesus, every horticulturalist paid a tax on the number of trees he owned, and if some of them were unproductive there was a definite loss sustained in allowing them to occupy space, take the fertility away from other trees, and otherwise encumber the ground. Thus, because an unproductive tree could not justify its existence, it was cut down and cast into the fire. But here again Jesus was not primarily interested in trees or vines or crops as such. He was far more interested in human beings—those creations formed in God's image, endowed with his attributes, and heirs to his glory.

Jesus set up the two final objectives for life when he said, first, ". . . wide is the gate, and broad is the way, that leadeth to destruction, and many there be which go in thereat," and second, "strait is the gate, and narrow is the way, which leadeth unto life, and few there be that find it." (Matthew 7:13-14.)

These two great objectives of life and death are still before us. Jesus gave us his opinion when he said, "Enter ye in at the strait gate." (Matthew 7:13.) That is our wisest idea, and yet most people approach these choices from the other direction.

Death may be said to come as a fraction. Sometimes while one is traveling down that broad road that leads to death, one allows his faith to die, his industry to die, his

34

courage to die, his morality to die, or his enthusiasm to die, and then only a part of him remains alive.

Recently while riding down the highway, I passed an old abandoned fruit orchard. Most of the trees were totally dead, their bare dry limbs reaching up into the sky like nature's skeletons. But over near the fence-line where the moisture was, the trees were uncared for but were green. And a few other trees were partially dead, with a few green leaves to indicate some life remaining. I wondered if that wasn't about the way we sometimes appear to God when we lack the abundance he intended us to have.

What an exciting challenge it is that we can, if we will, increase the abundance, the quality, and the happiness of our lives to the full measure set by the Master. His goal of abundance includes eternal progression, eternal glory, eternal happiness, and eternal love on as near a 100 percent basis as possible. To do this, we must multiply our abilities, our good works, and the spirit of our accomplishment so that our souls themselves may be increased in excellence.

A great line in the scripture says, "But the fruit of the Spirit is love, joy, peace, longsuffering, gentleness, goodness, faith, meekness, temperance: against such there is no law." (Galatians 5:22-23.) The Lord has given us this magnificent commission that we might be the vinedressers and the husbandmen controlling our own abundance. We are the pruners of our own vineyards, the fertilizers of our own soil, and the growers of the fruit that will be allotted to our own enjoyment.

In order to make the most of ourselves, we must make certain that all the wild branches are pruned out of our lives and that no damaging blight destroys the healthy leaves.

Elbert Hubbard once said, "I am looking out through the library window into the apple orchard and I see millions of blossoms that will never materialize or become fruit for lack of vitalization." The natural destiny of an apple blossom is that it should someday become an apple, and the planned destiny of a human soul is that it should someday become even as God. However, neither of these things will ever happen unless some vitalizing, fertilizing pollen is implanted in the right place at the right time.

It has always been a source of great delight for me to go into a large, well-ordered supermarket and see the great display of red apples, yellow peaches, blue plums, purple grapes, and deep red cherries with all their various flavors, vitamins, and colors that God himself designed to produce health, strength, vision, understanding, and wisdom in his children. I like to see those fruits that are all perfectly formed and brilliantly colored with their exquisite tastes and their ability to build up our human success.

The Lord has indicated that he expects us to produce in ourselves those far more important fruits of the spirit, including love, joy, peace, goodness, faith, and righteousness. Certainly these are the most profitable and pleasant of all crops. However, if we fail as good husbandmen, we may then produce the poisons of hate, bitterness, immorality, and dishonesty by default. There is an awful crop of evil that is presently overrunning our lands and sending a greater number of souls down the broad road that leads to death.

The other day a young housewife came to talk about some of the problems involved in being on the receiving end of some of this poisoned abundance. She is married to a man whose income does not provide what he wants his family to have. Therefore he has been supplementing his earned income with his thievery. When she remonstrated, he threatened her with her life if she told anyone. He has already been caught once and managed to alibi his way out of it. Of course she knows that sometime he will be caught again when his lying will not be successful. Then his whole family will pay the bitter price. But in the meantime, her suffering amounts to a kind of partial damnation. The wife prays that some miracle will touch her husband's distorted mind so that it will stop producing poisonous fruit. She wants his mind to produce the fruits of the spirit mentioned by Jesus. She wants him to understand something about the fruits of righteousness so that he may know that godliness is better than evil, and that industry is better than stealing.

Suppose we make a list of some of the fruits of the spirit that the Lord has recommended and that we would like to produce as the product of our personal husbandry. One of these would be genuine righteousness, which is the most profitable, the most pleasant, the most beautiful, the most strengthening of all of the fruits of the spirit. Or contemplate honesty with its high honor and its beautiful colors. And think how honesty shines out.

Another of the fruits of the spirit is love, that great emotion that makes us feel warm and happy inside. Another of the fruits of the spirit is a good conscience, which makes us feel our own lives are worthwhile. A good conscience gives us a peaceful spirit and a healthy, happy, aspiring soul.

On our list we should include all of those godly qualities that will make us radiant, happy, and faithful.

8
Jerusalem

One of the important centers of civilization down through our history has been the city of Jeusalem, with its related communities of Bethlehem, Bethany, Jericho, Emmaus, and Nazareth.

Abraham, who has much to do with building up this area, was born in approximately 2000 B.C. in Ur of the Chaldees, near the place where the Euphrates River empties into the Persian Gulf. Later he and his wife moved to Haran, near the headwaters of the Euphrates River and close to the northwestern corner of the Mediterranean Sea. There they lived for some time. Then the Lord appeared to Abraham and said to him:

"Get thee out of thy country, and from thy kindred, and from thy father's house, unto a land that I will shew thee:

"And I will make of thee a great nation, and I will bless thee, and make thy name great, and thou shalt be a blessing:

"And I will bless them that bless thee, and curse him that curseth thee: and in thee shall all families of the earth be blessed.

"So Abram departed, as the Lord had spoken unto him; and Lot went with him: and Abram was seventy and five years old when he departed out of Haran.

"And Abram took Sarai his wife, and Lot his brother's son, and all their substance that they had gathered, . . . and they went forth . . . into the land of Canaan. . . .

". . . And the Canaanite was then in the land." (Genesis 12:1-6.)

Abraham was later to be designated by the Lord as the father of the faithful. He located near what was later to become the city of Jerusalem. "And the Lord appeared unto

Abram, and said, Unto thy seed will I give this land: and there builded he an altar unto the Lord, who appeared unto him." (Genesis 12:7.)

"And the Lord said unto Abram, . . . Lift up now thine eyes, and look from the place where thou art northward, and southward, and eastward, and westward:

"For all the land which thou seest, to thee will I give it, and to thy seed for ever.

"And I will make thy seed as the dust of the earth: so that if a man can number the dust of the earth, then shall thy seed also be numbered. . . .

"Then Abram removed his tent, and came and dwelt in the plain of Mamre, which is in Hebron, and built there an altar unto the Lord." (Genesis 13:14-16, 18.)

"And Melchizedek king of Salem brought forth bread and wine: and he was the priest of the most high God.

"And he blessed him, and said, Blessed be Abram of the most high God, possessor of heaven and earth:

". . . And he gave him tithes of all." (Genesis 14:18-20.)

". . . the Lord made a covenant with Abram, saying, Unto thy seed have I given this land, from the river of Egypt into the great river, the river Euphrates." (Genesis 15:18.)

The posterity of Abraham was later held in captivity by the Egyptians for some four hundred years. After his children were released from their Egyptian bondage and after their forty years of wandering in the desert under Moses, they were restablished in the land that the Lord had given to Abraham.

When David became king about 1055 B.C., nearly one thousand years after the birth of Abraham, his headquarters was in Hebron. David was told by the Lord to drive out the idolatrous tribes, which he did. About 1000 B.C., David captured Salem, which was then merely a fortress, made it into his capital city, and changed its name to Jerusalem.

During some five hundred years after the reestablishment of the Israelites in their promised land, the only resources that they had to use as a temple were the little portable tabernacles they had carried with them as they wandered in the wilderness. They needed a temple and the Lord wanted them to have a temple. David was very anxious to build a temple and had accumulated a vast amount of wealth for that purpose.

The Lord denied David this ambition because he was a man of war. However, he was also a man of great loyalty, and God himself had referred to David as a "man after [God's] own heart." (Acts 13:22.) Later, David passed on to Solomon the job of building the temple, which he said he wanted to be of particular magnificence so that it would stand as a great symbol of the worship of God to all of the nations. David declared to Solomon:

"My son, as for me, it was in my mind to build an house unto the name of the Lord my God:

"But the word of the Lord came to me, saying, Thou hast shed blood abundantly, and hast made great wars: thou shalt not build an house unto my name, because thou hast shed much blood upon the earth in my sight.

"Behold, a son shall be born to thee, who shall be a man of rest; and I will give him rest from all his enemies round about: for his name shall be Solomon, and I will give peace and quietness unto Israel in his days. . . .

"Now, behold, in my trouble I have prepared for the house of the Lord an hundred thousand talents of gold, and a thousand thousand talents of silver; and of brass and iron without weight; for it is in abundance: timber also and stone have I prepared; and thou mayest add thereto.

"Moreover there are workmen with thee in abundance, hewers and workers of stone and timber, and all manner of cunning men for every manner of work." (1 Chronicles 22:7-9, 14-15.)

This amount of gold alone, according to the best estimate I can find, would have amounted at our price of gold today to some twenty billion dollars. In addition to the gold and silver, Solomon had gathered all kinds of costly jewels, fine woods, and other costly furnishings.

Sometime after David had been forbidden to build the temple, an angel of the Lord appeared to him and told him that the Lord desired him to build an altar on which to offer sacrifices to Jehovah. The altar was to be located in an elevated area used as a threshing floor in the middle of a wheat field owned by one of David's wealthy subjects, Ornan. David approached Ornan and told him what the angel had said and asked if Ornan would sell him the land. Ornan said that not only would the land be available, but he would also give it to David free of charge. Ornan offered to supply the materials to build the altar and also to furnish the wheat, oxen, and the oil that should make up the sacrifice. Then David said something extremely profound; he declared, "I will not offer unto the Lord an offering that doth cost me nothing." (See 1 Chronicles 21:18-27.)

The altar was built by David on this elevated area, which was also known as Mount Moriah. It was upon this same spot that Solomon later built his magnificent temple, which became one of the wonders of the world and the center of the worship of Jehovah on the earth.

Twenty years before the birth of Jesus, King Herod began rebuilding the temple. It was there that Jesus came to teach the wise men when he was twelve years old, and it was there that he made the center of his ministry.

On the last Tuesday of the Lord's life, which was the last day of his public ministry, he made his famous farewell speech to Jerusalem as he stood upon the Mount of Olives overlooking this area, which was endeared to every Jewish heart by the sacred memories which it contained. He said, "O Jerusalem, Jerusalem, thou that killest the prophets, and stonest them which are sent unto thee, how often would I have gathered thy children together, even as a hen gathereth her chickens under her wings, and ye would not! Behold, your house is left unto you desolate." (Matthew 23:37-38.)

Today Jerusalem still remains one of the great centers of the earth, with a great destiny. The temple will be rebuilt, and Jerusalem will be one of the capital cities of the Lord during his thousand-year millennial reign upon the earth.

This new city was described by John the Revelator, who saw it in a vision. He said it will be a city foursquare, twelve thousand furlongs in both length and breadth. Its walls will be rebuilt of jasper, and the city will be of pure gold, like unto clear glass. The foundations of the walls of the city will be garnished with all manner of precious stones: jasper, sapphires, chalcedony, emerald, sardonyx, sardius, chrysolite, beryl, topaz, chrysoprasus, jacinth, amethyst, and pearls. (See Revelation 21:16-21.)

"And the city [will have] no need of the sun, neither of the moon, to shine in it: for the glory of God did lighten it, and the Lamb is the light thereof.

"And the nations of them which are saved shall walk in the light of it: and the kings of the earth do bring their glory and honour into it.

"And the gates of it shall not be shut at all by day: for there shall be no night there.

"And they shall bring the glory and honour of the nations into it.

"And there shall in no wise enter into it any thing that defileth, neither whatsoever worketh abomination, or maketh a lie: but they which are written in the Lamb's book of life." (Revelation 21:23-27.)

The Revelator said of his vision:

"And he shewed me a pure river of water of life, clear as crystal, proceeding out of the throne of God and of the Lamb.

"In the midst of the street of it, on either side of the river, was there the tree of life, which bare twelve manner of fruits, and yielded her fruit every month: and the leaves of the tree were for the healing of the nations.

"And there shall be no more curse: but the throne of God and of the Lamb shall be in it; and his servants shall serve him:

"And they shall see his face; and his name shall be in their foreheads." (Revelation 22:1-4.)

Jerusalem has had a long, difficult history. It has been besieged, ransacked, and partially destroyed many times. Nebuchadnezzar captured the city in 586 B.C. and carried its people captive to Babylon, where they were enslaved for many years. King David sang the refrain of many generations when he said, "If I forget thee, O Jerusalem, let my right hand forget her cunning." (Psalm 137:5.) For many people throughout the world it is a center of pilgrimage—the Holy City, the earthly prototype of the heavenly Jerusalem.

Section 2

"If thou wilt do good, yea, and hold out faithful to the end, thou shalt be saved in the kingdom of God, which is the greatest of all the gifts of God; for there is no gift greater than the gift of salvation."
(*D&C 6:13.*)

Preparing Through Our Faith

9
Seek Ye First the Kingdom of God

In the greatest sermon that was ever preached, the greatest man who ever lived gave what was probably the wisest counsel that has ever been given. In the first part of the Sermon on the Mount, Jesus talked about loving one's enemies, of laying up treasures in heaven. He gave the Golden Rule and pointed out the wisdom of building one's house upon rock.

Matthew says: "He taught them as one having authority" (Matthew 7:29), and well he might, for he is the world's leading authority in spiritual affairs as well as its wisest counselor in every other field. In a nineteen-word formula, Jesus gave one of the basic principles of every accomplishment when he said, "But seek ye first the kingdom of God, and his righteousness; and all these things shall be added unto you." (Matthew 6:33.)

The scriptures refer to the kingdom of God with several different meanings. In one sense, the kingdom of God is a place; in another it identifies an organization; and in its third sense it describes a condition in the member.

On one occasion, Jesus said to the people, ". . . for, behold, the kingdom of God is within you." (Luke 17:21.) A footnote in the King James Version says he meant to say, "The kingdom of God is among you." He came to the earth and established his official organization for our benefit. When we speak of "building up the kingdom," we mean building up Christ's church. Jesus also referred to the kingdom of God as a condition. When he mentioned the kingdom of God he included the phrase "his righteousness," and righteousness is always a condition that refers to people.

Much of the benefit of belonging to God's kingdom is determined by how much of "his righteousness" finds its place in us. In this one phrase are embodied the attitudes, the virtues, the determinations, and the talents necessary to make us the great human beings that the Lord intended. In their natural order, *things* always follow talents. If we develop the talents or the abilities or the conditions within ourselves first, then the things will always follow.

President David O. McKay once said that the purpose of the Church is to change people, to make bad men good and good men better. The most important things that ever happen in our world are those changes that lift us upward toward God and our destiny.

William James once said, "The greatest discovery of my generation is that you can change your circumstances by changing your attitudes of mind." Everyone wants to change his circumstances but not very many are willing to change themselves. There are a lot more people who want to get into the church than there are who want to get the church into them.

Francis Bacon once said:

It is not what we eat but what we digest that makes us strong.
It is not what we earn but what we save that makes us rich.
It is not what we read but what we remember that makes us learned.
It is not what we think but what we do that makes us successful.
It is not what we preach but what we practice that makes us Christians.

The dictionary defines *righteousness* as "the state of being upright." It implies a solid character, an acceptance of correct principles supported by the kind of conduct that would win the favor and approval of God. The opposite of righteousness is wickedness. Wickedness is transgression, a violation of law. Unrighteousness is rebellion against God. It tends to tear down God's establishment, and the violation of any divine law always leads us toward unhappiness.

The primary reasons for failure are illustrated by a survey made some time ago at Stanford University to determine the reasons why some people lost their jobs. It was discovered that of all those who had been discharged from their employment, 94 percent of the dismissals were for reasons not even remotely connected with job competence. These reasons included dishonesty, immorality, idleness, or other breakdowns in righteousness. These people were trying to get the *things* without the *talents*. Anyone is loading himself up with some severe handicaps when he ignores the divine formula, ". . . seek ye *first* the kingdom of God, and his righteousness, and all these *things* shall be added unto you." (Italics added.)

It is far more difficult to be successful when one is loaded down with so much evil that he is untrustworthy, profane, drunken, immoral, dishonest, or selfish, for all of the unrighteous traits are instruments of failure and death. Evil is the opposite of right, the opposite of success, the opposite of happiness. Sometimes we miss the boat by just reversing the order given by the Master so that we seek the *things* first. Many people feel that the Church and its religious activities are something that can be attended to later on in life, when they have nothing else to do, so they begin looking for things and pleasures first, whereas this divine law says that we should build the necessary character, wisdom, industry, and godliness into our lives *first*.

The traits of character, righteousness, and industry will work wonders in our business affairs, politics, personal relationships, finances, and education, as well as religion. If we can just get our membership in God's kingdom in the right order, then everything else will follow.

Recently a very attractive young woman was discussing her problems. Like everyone else she wanted the good things in life. She wanted a happy home, the joys of loved ones, and faithful friends. But instead of seeking the kingdom of God and his righteousness first, she wanted the joys first, so that in her search she was without the guidance and benefit of the sound principles of the gospel. It was therefore perfectly natural that she soon started making a lot of unnecessary mistakes. Her character became pitted and pocked with ugliness, sin, and immorality, and she has become a slave to her own mistakes.

She is perfectly aware that she is going in the wrong direction and she wonders where she is going to end up. It is now very difficult for her to seek the kingdom of God. She asks herself why she continues to do as she does, and she claims that she herself doesn't know the answer. She is beginning to get the feeling that she is so bogged down with discouragement and failure that she is rapidly reaching the point of no return. Many people actually seek the kingdom of God last in a kind of weak deathbed repentance after their lives are actually over.

It is so much more expensive and so much less satisfactory to try to remodel an old building than it is to built it to the right specifications in the first place. A sixty-four-year-old man recently came in to talk about his problems. All of his life he had been trying to get the benefits without the talents and the industry. In disregarding the righteousness part of the formula, he had made almost every mistake. He said, "If I had known forty years ago what I know now, I would have done differently." Then he said, "I wish I could live my life over again."

How ridiculous can we be? No one can live his life over again. There are no rehearsals in life. We can't rehearse birth or death. We can't try out marriage or medicine or engineering or life. Neither can we always be tearing down and starting over. If this man had followed the formula given by Jesus, he would have known forty years ago what he knows now, and then it would have been much easier to carry it out. This man would now like to remodel his life, change his attitudes, his procedures, his habits, get a new set of friends, turn back his calendar, and be born again. However, some of these things are now much too difficult. Many young people who think that it is difficult to live the gospel when they are young will find it is much more difficult when they try to remodel themselves later on. How much better it is if, when we are young, we apply the formula of Jesus: ". . . seek ye first the kingdom of God, and his righteousness; and all these things shall be added unto you."

The Lord has set us a perfect example of righteousness. He was the great teacher, the great doer. Men called him Master, and God the Father was pleased with him. The more that we become like him, the more successful and the more happy we will be. If we make ourselves acceptable to him, we cannot fail to be acceptable to his laws. Every unrighteous thought or act works against us, no matter in what field we may be interested. We should not only seek the kingdom of God, but we should seek it first.

As we base our lives on evil in any degree, it always becomes more and more difficult to change, until finally we may become like Satan, and repentance becomes impossible. As our righteousness dies little by little, we have less and less to work with. Our lives are short even at their best. With the most reliable road maps and no detours, we will have to hurry to reach our destination on time. How much more satisfactory and profitable it is when we come into possession of our good resolutions and determinations at the beginning of our lives rather than at their end.

According to our present schedule, only a few are traveling that straight and narrow path that leads to the celestial kingdom. They are the ones who are valiant in the testimony of Jesus. How intense, then, will be the wail of those who fail and say, "I wish I could live my life over again."

Certainly the most tragic waste in the world is not in the devastations that go with war; it isn't the cost of crime; it isn't the erosion of our soils, or the depletion of our raw materials, or the loss of our gold supply. The greatest waste is that human beings, you and I, live so far below the level of our possibilities. Compared with what God intended us to be, we are only partly alive. Sin and failure always leave their marks upon our souls for both here and hereafter.

And so we come back again to this basic law given by the greatest intelligence of heaven, who said, ". . . see ye first the kingdom of God, and his righteousness; and all these things shall be added unto you." What a wonderful philosophy on which to build a happy, prosperous life for both here and hereafter. May God bless us that we may not only seek and find, but also fully identify ourselves with his kingdom and help to establish his righteousness upon the earth.

10
Hold Up Your Hands

In the true church of Christ we have the thrilling, exciting experience of holding up our hands and making personal covenants with the Lord that we will sustain and support those who are placed in authority over us.

The Lord placed in our hands the responsibility for working out our eternal exaltation before him. When we are sick, hands are placed upon our heads and we are given blessings for the restoration of our health. Members of the Church are confirmed by the laying on of hands. By the laying on of hands men are ordained to the priesthood and persons are set apart for that portion of the work of the Lord that they are called to perform. We raise our hands in salute; we hold them over our hearts as we pledge allegiance to the flag. We clasp hands in friendship and fellowship. We lay hands upon the shoulders of our friends to give commendation and encouragement. With a pair of willing, ambitious, capable, clean hands we can move mountains and we can save souls.

The story is told of a young man who went blind in his early youth. Many years later after an operation, the first thing that his newly restored vision rested upon was his own hand, and he thought he had never imagined anything quite so wonderful as this great human resource with its own circulation system, communication system, temperature control, self-healing ability, and wonderful covering of skin.

Think of the usefulness of fingers. They can readily be trained to play the piano, dial telephone numbers, and do accounting.

The ancient Israelites had a custom of wearing phylacteries. The Lord knew then what every one of us ought to know now—that certain passages in the scriptures must never be forgotten if we are to be successful. Therefore, to help the people remember, he required that they write some of these passages down on pieces of parchment, encase them in little leather tubes, and bind them across their foreheads and between their eyes. They were required to hang them around their necks and bind them on their arms like wristwatches and wear them like rings upon their fingers. About this custom the Lord said to the people:

"And these words, which I command thee this day, shall be in thine heart:

"And thou shalt teach them diligently unto thy children, and shalt talk of them when thou sittest in thine house, and when thou walkest by the way, and when thou liest down, and when thou risest up.

"And thou shalt bind them for a sign upon thine hand, and they shall be as frontlets between thine eyes." (Deuteronomy 6:6-8.)

Mothers sometimes make an interesting adaptation of this idea. When they send us on an important errand, the purpose of which they do not want us to forget, they help us remember by tying pieces of string on our fingers so that no matter where we go or what we do we will remember what they want us to do. That is somewhat like what the Lord did to the children of Israel, and when I raise my hand to make a personal covenant with the Lord, I try to imagine which phylacteries he would most like to see on my hand. Here are some of the things I have been thinking about.

The first finger on the hand is the thumb, which serves as the anchor of the hand. It stands for knowledge. Jesus said, "And this is life eternal, that they might know thee the only true God, and Jesus Christ, whom thou hast sent." (John 17:3.)

Dr. Henry C. Link once pointed out that "nothing puts so much order into human life as to live by a set of sound principles." The soundest principles are the principles of the gospel of Jesus Christ. However, before we can live by them effectively, we must know what they are.

The second finger is the pointing finger. This is the finger we use to show the way. This is our directing finger. We must be converts before we can be disciples. We must be converts before we can be missionaries. We must be converts before we can be leaders. We must be converts before we can show others the way. Jesus said to Peter, "Simon, . . . when thou art converted, strengthen thy brethren." (Luke 22:31-32.) Peter may have been a little bit offended at this, for he probably felt that as the chief apostle, he was already converted. But what happened that very night at the house of Caiphas when Peter denied the Lord three times may have indicated that even he was not fully converted. It would help each of us if we were to have strong, well-worked-out convictions centered in us.

The third finger is the power finger. It has the central location on the hand. It reminds us that we must WANT to succeed—in capital letters. If we want to succeed in letters an inch high, we will fail, but if we want to succeed in letters a yard high, then we will succeed.

The Lord said, "Therefore, if ye have desires to serve God ye are called to the work." (D&C 4:3.) If we don't *want* to do it, we *can't* do it. Alma said that God grants "unto men according to their desire. . . ." (Alma 29:4.) We ought to spend a lot more time than we ordinarily do in increasing the volume and intensity of our righteous desires. We must really WANT to be disciples of Christ; we must really WANT to be servants of the Master.

The fourth finger is the ring finger. This is the finger that signifies our falling in love. This is the family finger. This is the finger that represents the source of our satisfactions and our eternal happiness for both here and hereafter. Shakespeare said, "No profit comes where there is no pleasure taken." We can't do very well that which we don't enjoy doing. If we don't get great pleasure out of our families, we should repent, because we are doing something wrong.

The last finger is the little finger, the weakest finger. It is the finger that has the poorest position on the hand, and we might imagine that we could just take it off the team and throw it away without losing very much. However, the big finger cannot say to the little finger, "I have no need of thee." The little finger may come at the end of the line-up but that is the quarterback position, and we don't need a great big man to be quarterback, providing the other mem-

54

bers of the team are fully qualified and effectively functioning. The thumb knows its business backwards and forwards; the pointing finger has some powerful, well-developed convictions; the middle finger WANTS to function in capital letters; and the ring finger gets great satisfaction from its work. The little finger is the worker. It is the one that takes care of the mechanics of production, the one that handles the checkup and does the follow-through. It represents the one James referred to when he pleaded for "doers of the word" and not just hearers and talkers only.

Someone has said, "My, oh my, what miracles we could accomplish if our hands moved as fast as our tongues. After all is said and done, there is usually a lot more said than done."

If I had the gift of speech and the power to plant a conviction that I would like to have, I would say to the millions of people in the world who are earnestly seeking to be disciples of the Master, "Hold up your hands to God and make a solemn covenant with him to keep all of his commandments." I would remind every one of that thrilling occasion when Moses was leading the children of Israel in their battle against the Amalekites. He took the rod of God in his hands and went to the top of a sacred mount, where he held up his hands to God. As long as Moses held up his hands, Israel prevailed, but when he let his hands down, the Amalekites prevailed. As his arms became heavy with weariness, Aaron and Hur stood on either side of him and helped him to hold up his hands until the battle was won.

If we all hold up clean, honest, industrious hands to God, his work will prevail. May all of us together effectively hold up our hands to God so that we and our covenants may be acceptable to him.

11
Be of Good Cheer

We live in a world of the greatest wonders and miracles. It is filled with the most ample abundance and abounds in exquisite beauty. Our world is a place where religion, science, art, and opportunity may be endlessly fostered. On the sixth day of creation, God brought forth his greatest masterpiece—man—formed in his own image. Then God put all things under the feet of man and gave him lasting dominion over everything upon the earth, including himself.

Man possesses the highest order of intelligence in the world. He also has the most glorious possibilities for everlasting happiness and eternal exaltation. Job said: "But there is a spirit in man: and the inspiration of the Almighty giveth them understanding." (Job 32:8.)

At his best, man is made up of the most godly qualities, including faith, character, spirit, ability, love, devotion, and righteousness. And as one of the finishing touches for this great human personality, the Creator endowed him with the faculty for joy. Joy is a quality that adds luster to one's own soul and also lifts up others and makes them feel at their best. More than about any other, this is the trait that brightens the soul and makes life beautiful.

I believe it would be pretty difficult to ever have an abundance of life without an abundance of joy. For what would any kind of abundance be like if one could not laugh and sing and shout for joy?

The skylark is a symbol of happiness and high purpose. It has been said that no bird equals the skylark in heart or voice. In a still hour you can hear its thrilling notes at nearly a mile's distance. Long after its form is lost to sight, it still floods a thousand acres of sky with song. The movement of the skylark is swift and sure. In almost perpendicular flight it rises quickly toward the sky. It seems to be lifted up by the ecstasy of its own happy heart. On the earth the skylark seems timid, silent, and unsure of itself. It has little color, feature, or form to recommend it. Its inspiration comes when it is soaring and pouring out its rapturous song in a flood of shrill delight.

Certainly it was intended that God's greatest creation should have an abundance of the spirit of the skylark. A happier song leads to greater accomplishment. The inspiration of genuine happiness enlarges our vision and increases our pulse rate. It is an antidote for boredom. It is a deterrent to sin and a preventative of negative living. It is highly contagious. As one songwriter has pointed out, "A heart can inspire other hearts with its fire."

Jesus was aware of the need for joy in our lives, for he went around saying to people, "Be of good cheer. . . ." (Matthew 14:27.) He said, "Why are ye troubled? and why do thoughts arise in your hearts?" (Luke 24:38.) "Rejoice, and be exceeding glad." (Matthew 5:12.) The scriptures refer to eternal happiness, the songs of the angels, and the great rejoicing that takes place in heaven over righteousness.

The purpose of the gospel is to bring to men the greatest happiness. That is also the chief end of life. One of our scriptures says, ". . . men are, that they might have joy." (2 Nephi 2:25.) And Jesus said, ". . . I have spoken unto you . . . that your joy might be full." (John 15:11.) Solomon pointed out that "a merry heart doeth good like a medicine." (Proverbs 17:22.) A merry heart also contains one of the finest beauty treatments. Cheerfulness puts enthusiasm in one's heart, a twinkle in his eye, a glow on his face, and a radiance into his soul.

Abraham Lincoln was once urged by a senator to appoint a certain man as postmaster. But after the interview, President Lincoln turned him down. The senator asked him why. President Lincoln said, "I did not like his face." The senator said, "You can't hold the poor man responsible for his face." But President Lincoln said, "Everyone is responsible for his face." And everyone is responsible for his attitude, his faith, his industry, his dress, his posture, the spring in his step, his honesty, his disposition, and the effect he has on other people.

To make people happy is one of the main duties of life, and to foster gloom, depression, and loneliness is one of its greatest sins. Actually, happiness is not an easy accomplishment. Like every other success, happiness is based on obedience to the divine laws of the universe.

No one can do wrong and feel right. Some people try to have a good time by getting drunk, taking dope, or through immoral acts. But drunkards are not happy, dope addicts are not happy, immoral people are not happy. Satan, the instigator of evil, is a very unhappy person, and he seeks that all men might be miserable like unto himself.

Happiness requires that we be expert in inspiring confidence and love in those around us, particularly in our family members.

Joy is not only a reward of righteousness, it is also an expectation of good. Jesus said, "It is more blessed to give than to receive." (Acts 20:35.) When we give joy, we receive it back multiplied. We live in a world of opposites. All around us we see the contrasts of good and bad, right and wrong, success and failure. And the ennobling quality of good cheer also has some opposites.

Righteousness always brings joy, and sin always brings misery. A dejected mind causes one to feel forlorn, melancholy, and have attitudes of hopelessness. What is more unpleasant than a dark, gloomy, ugly depressing person? Some people become actual dispensers of gloom. They are spreaders of melancholia and producers of sorrow and heartbreak. They are the opposites of the skylark. When we do evil, we have an unpleasant outlook on life; we become pessimistic and expect nothing but tragedy.

A most uncomplimentary title used to describe people is killjoy. On the other hand, what is more pleasant than to be a happy person—one who has an honest inner radiance, one who is good company, one who has a merry heart and an inspiring personality?

Many years ago I was employed on a farm by a man whom I'll never forget. Sometimes I used to stay out on the dry farm for a week at a time without seeing any other human being except for one visit by him. I would take a large enough load of hay to feed my horses for a week and enough food to last me for three days. Then in the middle of the week my employer would bring food to carry me over the last three days of the week. As the time approached when I expected him to arrive, I used to have the pleasantest feelings of expectation. I was very glad to see him, not only for the bread and meat that he brought, but for his joyous attitude, which lifted me up and vitalized my whole person.

On these occasions I learned something about the meaning of the statement of Jesus when he said, "Man shall not live by bread alone." (Matthew 4:4.) As long as this man lived I never knew him to be unhappy or sad, depressed, or negative. I am sure that things did not always go as he wanted them to, but he always made the most of the good things and the least of everything else. He was always positive, always cheerful. He was like a skylark. He was enthusiastic about life; he was enthusiastic about conditions and people. He was even enthusiastic about me and the work I did for him. This attitude automatically made me a better workman and a better person.

Being with some people is like sitting around a cheerful fire with pleasant company, or enjoying a good meal in an inspiring environment of sights and sounds. Good cheer beautifies the countenance, gladdens the heart, cleanses the soul, raises the spirits, refreshes the enthusiasm, brightens the appearance, and gives one a warm, friendly disposition. What a great accomplishment when a good husband can bring real joy to the heart of his wife so that it lights up her eyes with radiance just to be near him! And how great is that father who can bring joy and enthusiasm into the hearts of his children so that they will be inspired to do righteously—to love truth and to feel the warm fire of happiness and a sense of spiritual well-being in the depths of their souls.

Joy uplifts everyone. Just think of the great opportunity we have to please God and to make him happy. And who can think of any of his commandments that are more important than the one in which the Master says, "Be of good cheer." (Matthew 14:27.)

12
Endowed Sermons

The other day I read an interesting story about Sir John Gayer who, some three hundred years ago, was Lord Mayor of London. On one occasion while on an expedition to Algeria, he became separated from his caravan, and while he was without any means of protecting himself, he met a great African lion face to face. Because he was very frightened and feared that this wild beast might destroy his life, he made a vow to the Lord that if the Lord would protect him from the lion, he would give all of the profits from his Algerian expedition to the church. The lion finally went his way and allowed Sir John to get back to his camp safe and sound.

When the Lord Mayor returned to London, he faithfully kept his promise and turned over to the church the two hundred pounds that he had earned for the purpose of financing an annual sermon observing his deliverance from the lion. The income and honor that this endowment produced was great enough to motivate many ministers to vie with each other in improving their preaching so that they might be chosen to deliver the annual lion sermon. And so year after year this practice has been continued. Even today the lion sermon is one of the best known of the endowed sermons given in English churches.

There is another sermon called "The Storm Sermon," which commemorates the escape of Joseph Taylor of Paternoster Row from the great storm of 1703. There is also a sermon commemorating England's escape from the gunpowder plottings by Guy Fawkes. Still another sermon gives thanks for the dispersion of the Spanish Armada. Another endowment was established in the early 1700s and requires the governors of Christ's Hospital to attend an annual sermon in Surrey village whether it is convenient or not; if those responsible for the hospital do not attend this particular sermon, the institution will lose the five thousand pounds bequeathed to it. In 1937 the will of the Reverend

E.S.G. Savile provided the funds for the Oxford Church of Christ to select a preacher and pay him three hundred pounds to deliver a sermon on the text "Thy Kingdom Come." The sermon must be delivered and printed in book form before the preacher receives his money.

The sponsors of these endowed sermons have seemed very anxious that the public be regularly reminded of some particular idea they feel to be important.

We have many other kinds of endowed lectures. Back in the beginning of this century, A. Lawrence Lowe was the president of Harvard University. A group of his admirers established an endowment, the interest from which would pay a specially selected person one thousand dollars each year to give the annual Lowe lecture in which President Lowe was honored and his work extolled. Harvard also has a Phi Beta Kappa lecture, which has been in existence since about 1790. Many people with wealth have endowed university chairs so that a professor can be employed for an entire year. Harvard has five hundred chairs that have been thus endowed.

This custom of setting up endowments to perpetuate ideas has many useful applications. With the changing times and changing ways of life, some parts of our culture might be completely forgotten if someone were not paid to regularly remind us about it.

The Bible mentions entire books of scripture that we presently know nothing about. As civilizations have been destroyed, much of their accumulated knowledge has been lost. A lot of our important scientific research is no longer available.

God himself has given some instructions that might be considered as endowed sermons. The scriptures themselves have cost the lives of many of the greatest prophets. Jesus and most of his apostles gave their lives that we might receive his message of salvation. Certainly that was a much larger endowment than the two hundred pounds that maintains the lion lecture.

Many years after the crucifixion and the violent deaths of the apostles, the resurrected Jesus appeared to John the

61

Revelator on the Isle of Patmos and gave him a vision of some of the important events that would take place in our world at a date that is still in the future. As the Lord prepared to give this revelation, he said to the Revelator: "What thou seest, write in a book. . . ." (Revelation 1:11.) By this process the Lord hoped to get the substance of this revelation into the hands of as many people as possible. Therefore, while John was still in the spirit he wrote the message down, and as a consequence we now have this important information in a way as close as possible to the way the Lord originally gave it.

Jesus was commissioned by his Father to preach one of the greatest sermons ever given, in what we know as the Sermon on the Mount. This was also put in written form for our benefit, and the best way for us to make its meaning profitable is for us to preach it to ourselves.

Preaching is one of the areas where it may be more blessed to give than to receive. One of the purposes for which the Lord equipped us with powers of reason, meditation, and the ability to think and absorb the printed page is so that we may not be too dependent upon others. The way to get the most out of any idea is to study it, think it through, analyze it, discover its purpose, and then make some decisions about it. Then we can organize it and become enthusiastic about it. The substance of ideas can be so organized as to produce enthusiasm in us.

Now just suppose that you had been appointed to give a very important sermon next year. And suppose that if you did it well, you would receive a large material reward and great public honor. Undoubtedly you would want to understand its message thoroughly and spend a lot of time in preparing to give it effectively. If you have strong convictions about it, based on facts, you could probably improve the lives of many other people.

Actually, that is similar to what our situation is. Jesus endowed his apostles with authority, and in his last post-mortal message he gave them this commission, which also comes to us:

"Go ye therefore, and teach all nations, baptizing them in the name of the Father, and of the Son, and of the Holy Ghost:

"Teaching them to observe all things whatsoever I have commanded you: and, lo, I am with you alway, even unto the end of the world." (Matthew 28:19-20.)

Just as the Master's mission was to help us, so our mission is to help each other. He has given some messages for us to give our families and our neighbors. He has endowed us with gifts of intelligence, personality, and faith so that we can help others.

A young man who had recently returned from military service told of an interesting experience where a fellow soldier sought him out and said, "Bill, preach to me." Bill said, "What do you mean?" His friend said, "I would like to have you preach to me. You are different from the other soldiers that I am acquainted with, and I would like to find out more about you and what has made you what you are." Bill was endowed with faith and with great character qualities that were already preaching sermons. And his friend said, "If you will preach to me, I may be able to become like you are."

Over our lifetime each of us is endowing a sermon by which we can make someone else better. The Lord has set up some endowments for the purpose of rewarding us. He has made it very profitable to be the deliverer of his messages. For example, in June 1829, he gave a revelation to John Whitmer in which he said:

"Hearken, my servant John, and listen to the words of Jesus Christ, your Lord and your Redeemer.

"For behold, I speak unto you with sharpness and with power, for mine arm is all over the earth.

"And I will tell you that which no man knoweth save me and thee alone—

"For many times you have desired of me to know that which would be of the most worth unto you.

"Behold, blessed are you for this thing, and for speaking my words which I have given you according to my commandments.

"And now, behold, I say unto you that the thing which will be of the most worth unto you will be to declare repentance unto this people, that you may bring souls unto me, that you may rest with them in the kingdom of my Father." (D&C 15.)

The Lord told Joseph Smith, Oliver Cowdery, and David Whitmer:

"Remember the worth of souls is great in the sight of God. . . .

"Wherefore, you are called to cry repentance unto this people.

"And if it so be that you should labor all your days in crying repentance unto this people, and bring, save it be one soul unto me, how great shall be your joy with him in the kingdom of my Father!

"And now, if your joy will be great with one soul that you have brought unto me into the kingdom of my Father, how great will be your joy if you should bring many souls unto me!" (D&C 18:10, 14-16.)

Jesus compared the worth of a soul to the wealth of all the earth. I don't know just how much the earth might be worth; however, I recently read a newspaper article that gave the assessed valuation of just one section of the United States alone as being over one trillion dollars. And with the right kind of communication from us, backed up with the right kind of industry, many trillion-dollar souls could be saved.

When it is our own souls that are being saved, it makes a difference, but what about our children's souls, and those of our grandchildren? And what about our neighbors, and what about those who would be our best friends if we only knew them? Certainly a most profitable undertaking for us personally is to have a part in that great enterprise in which God himself is engaged.

The Master said to a group of fishermen, "Follow me, and I will make you fishers of men." (Matthew 4:19.) He has endowed our lives themselves so that they can preach the greatest sermons. When we match this endowment with our own good works, enriched by the holy scriptures, then we may be effective co-venturers in that great enterprise in which God himself spends his entire time.

13
I Had a Friend

When Robert Louis Stevenson was once asked the secret of his radiant, useful life, he replied, "I had a friend." He did not say who his friend was or what he had done to deserve having this benefit lavished upon him. However, regardless of who or what or how, one of the greatest of all the secrets of happiness comes from our ability to make solid, uplifting, genuine friends.

William Shakspeare indicated the value of this ability when he said:

> Those friends thou hast, and their adoption tried,
> Grapple them to thy soul with hoops of steel.
> —*Hamlet,* Act 1, scene 3

One of the important places to start in any undertaking is to give effective consideration to those abilities and skills by which we bring about the most worthwhile benefits. This applies not only to friendships with people, but also to friendships with ideas, attitudes, and personality traits.

Abraham Lincoln accounted for his own success somewhat as Robert Louis Stevenson had done. Lincoln named his best friend when he said, "All that I am or ever hope to be I owe to my angel mother." Father Abraham had two distinctive titles. He was called the "Friend of God" (James 2:23) and "the father of the faithful."

The Savior has encouraged us in the highest kind of ambitions by inviting our friendship with his own life. To a chosen group he said, "Henceforth I call you not servants; . . . but I have called you friends. . . ." (John 15:15.) He gave a rather exciting basis for this particular relationship when he said, "Ye are my friends, if ye do whatsoever I command you." (John 15:14.) To keep his commandments insures the highest level of conduct.

Certainly the most important basis for any real friendship is a mutual interest, a common respect, a unity of objective. One man said that he not only believed in God, but he also agreed with him. This agreement or obedience or union of purpose offers the most profound basis for a pleasant and profitable association. Of course, the right to any great relationship must be earned and continually deserved. This applies not only to our friendship with God, but also to our friendship with good ideas.

Abraham's father was an idol worshiper. Abraham himself was surrounded by evil and unrighteous practices; but he had something much better in mind than friendship with evil. He was not one of those mentioned in the scripture who loved Satan more than God. He not only loved God; he also loved good. He loved accomplishment and happiness. He loved those things that were important to God. And to help Abraham foster more enobling friendships, God said to him, "Abraham, get thee out of thy country, and from thy kindred, and from thy father's house, unto a land that I will show thee." (Abraham 2:3.) The Lord wanted Abraham to live in an area that was more congenial, more righteous, one that would provide a good life for Abraham and his posterity.

God created man as a gregarious being, and we do our best when we are associated with and work together with those nations, communities, businesses, and families with which we share similar interests and with which we have congenial backgrounds and attitudes. It is also helpful to have common ideals and disciplined companionship.

In great literature our finest authors have created some of the most worthwhile companionships. And by becoming familiar with the great ideas, including the great scriptures, we establish in ourselves the necessary disciplines and put our lives in harmony with the best thoughts and feelings that have ever existed.

Friendliness is the most pleasant and the most productive when it becomes part of us. We should also bind to us great ideas and stimulating standards that also become our friends and make us friendly. We should surround ourselves with friends on the inside as well as on the outside. We may become a staunch friend of reason, of righteousness, of generosity, of courage, of greatness. All important character

67

qualities give us strength and power. Through our friendship with great virtues and ambitions we may attract to ourselves the pleasantest experiences, the greatest beauty, and the finest accomplishments.

The Lord does not expect us to go through life alone; he gives us this companionship of virtues. The poet Joyce Kilmer said:

> Because the way was long and hard
> And through a lone and dreary land,
> God placed upon my lips a song
> And put a lantern in my hand.

The dictionary describes a friend as a promoter, a well-wisher who seeks our society and welfare. How fortunate is he who can look up to God, to his country, to his family, and to truth, and can say, with Robert Louis Stevenson, "I had a friend."

14
Gratitude

We have an interesting custom among us where we set aside special days to think about special things, and one of the greatest of these days is a day that we call Thanksgiving. This is a day in which we express our gratitude for life's many benefits. Cicero, the old Roman statesman, once said that gratitude was the mother of virtues.

How happy we ought to be that we can be as thankful as we desire! We are grateful *to* God, but we should also be grateful *for* God. He is the author of our lives, the designer of our faith, a fulfiller of promises. As he has sown, so we shall reap. God serves in the very high office as our provider. He gave us this earth and all that goes with it. And as our eternal Heavenly Father, he has also given us ourselves. Our greatest blessing is that according to the natural laws of heredity, we may share the destiny of him who begat us in his own image.

In his infinite wisdom God has provided for us the most profitable way of life. His godly program always produces happiness and eternal godliness in all of those who follow it. However, the blessing that each of us should probably be more grateful for than all others is ourself. It might sound a little bit selfish to go before God with our Thanksgiving Day prayers and say, "I am grateful for me." But if this is selfishness, at least it is a very intelligent selfishness. He has given us dominion, and he has decreed that almost everything in our individual lives depends upon us. No one can do very much for anyone else until he has first done something for himself. Certainly the first soul that anyone should bring to God is his own soul. We can't teach something to someone else until we first learn it ourselves. From every point of view, how extremely fortunate we are that God has given us the superb gift of ourselves. He has given us a life of tremendous importance, an unlimited potential intelligence, and an all-powerful industry that we may exercise endlessly in our own behalf.

Many of the greatest success words in our language include the powerful little word *self,* such as self-development, self-discovery, self-confidence, self-analysis, self-respect, self-motivation, self-education, self-discipline, self-esteem, self-expression, self-help, self-composure, self-starter, self-defense, and self-control. How grateful we ought to be that God has placed each of us in charge of our own eternal success and has imposed upon us absolutely no limitations, and no one can help us much except ourselves. Only we can build up our own muscles, vitalize our own faith, develop our own courage, generate our own industry, determine our own efficiency, and establish our own character and spirituality; and no one can even help us if he doesn't also have our cooperation. However, each one of us is allowed to intervene endlessly, continually, and eternally in any of our own interests.

We are the managers of our own destiny. We may be abandoned by our friends or opposed by our enemies, but these will have minimum effect if we work endlessly, enthusiastically, and effectively to bring about justice and promote our own welfare.

Governments, religion, laws, and all of the resources of the universe were made for the benefit of man. Jesus once said that even the sabbath was made for man and not man for the sabbath. (See Mark 2:24.) By our own industry, study, and prayer, we can build faith and do almost every other worthwhile thing in the world. We can even obligate God to serve us, for the Savior has said, "I, the Lord, am bound when ye do what I say. . . ." (D&C 82:10.) How unfortunate are they who have to depend on others because they have no self-analyzing ability, no self-discipline, no self-control, and too many bad attitudes.

A fine young salesman was once telling me about his discouragement. I was a little amazed at the fact that in spite of his potentiality, he had so many bills and so little money. But some negative attitudes had gotten hold of him that had thrown him into a paralyzing depression. Instead of counting his blessings and focusing his mind on his opportunities, he was hoarding his glooms and centering his fears on all of the reasons why he should fail. I got a piece of paper and suggested that we make a list of his assets. He felt that he worked for the greatest company in the world. He sold a wonderful product. When he was successful, he rendered excellent service to people. He lived in the greatest country in the world. He had a fine family. He was young and enjoyed good health.

After he thought the list was complete, I suggested to him that he had left out what was by far his most important asset. He could not think what it might be. Then I asked him to try to think of something more important than the fact that if he wanted to, he could get himself on his side. He had a tremendous resource available to himself that he was not counting on or using. I quoted to him what the great Harvard psychologist, William James, said: "The greatest discovery of my generation is that you can change your circumstances by changing your attitudes of mind." What this young salesman needed was to change himself—to change his attitudes and work on becoming unselfish, concerned about others, friendly, and helpful.

I said to my friend, "The only one who can prevent you from being the greatest salesman in your company is you." The greatest responsibility that God has ever laid upon the shoulders of any man is to make the best and the most of his own life.

When I was born, God did not place primary responsibility for my welfare upon the president of the United States or the president of the Church or the governor of my state. He placed it upon me. He provided two parents to help me get started and assist me to the age of responsibility, but sometime along the line the job had to be turned over to me. This should be great news to us, for there is no one else in the world who could possibly be half as interested in me as I am. Besides that, I would far rather take orders from me than from anyone else. How grateful I am for me and that God has given me an unlimited dominion over myself!

Abraham Lincoln once said that everyone is about as happy as he makes up his mind to be. And so, in expressing our thanks to God on Thanksgiving Day or any other day, we might say, "I am grateful for me. I am grateful that you put me in charge of my own development and my own eternal salvation and gave me unlimited and unrestricted powers to make of myself the finest kind of person for both here and hereafter."

15
The Vanishing Point

The other day I studied some of the forty-four different definitions of the little five-letter word *point*. The dictionary said that a point was the tip or the end of some tapering object, such as a pencil or a sword or a pin. It also indicated that there are a great many things that come to a point. There is a boiling point and a freezing point. We know of some geographical high points and low points. People also have points. Some people have many good points while others have bad points. We have points of interest and points of departure and points of arrival. We may get so far out in life that we go beyond the point of no return.

Sometimes we miss the main point in our lives or in our education or in our religion. Perhaps our logic has no point, or we ourselves never quite reach the point designated by our projected success. When we do a lot of things without some particular point in mind, our lives may lose much of their significance and become pointless. Sometimes we taper off in our industry or in our faith, or we allow ourselves to slip to such a low point in our logic or in our thinking or in our conduct that our accomplishment disappears beyond the vanishing point.

We are all aware of optical illusions that bother us because of the deception that gets into our perspective. For example, if we look down a long row of telephone poles, the one by which we are standing seems very large and impressive while the one on the distant horizon seems like just a pinpoint. That actually seems to be true. Our eyes tell us that it is true, and yet it is not true. We can prove the point for ourselves by getting into an automobile and riding to that vanishing point on the horizon for a closer inspection. Our eyes will then tell us that the telephone pole by which we are now standing has suddenly become the most important telephone pole in the entire system, and the one that we formerly thought so impressive has now lost almost all of its importance.

If we look down a railroad track, the rails seem to get closer and closer together as they get farther from our eyes, and finally the rails seem to run together so that instead of two rails, it seems there is now only one rail. This deception in perspective makes everything close by seem of great consequence and everything in the distance seem of little importance. If we were to put a nickle over our eye, it would blot out the greatest star a few hundred million miles away. A quarter will blot out the sun. However, that is not a sign that the quarter is larger than the sun; it is just closer to our eye.

Sometime ago I flew over the city of Chicago, and from where I sat, my eyes told me that not one of the great skyscrapers there was more than one-half inch high, and yet I knew that I was being deceived. This interesting phenomenon applies not only to distance; it applies also to time. If you would like to perform an interesting experiment, just ask a six-year-old which he would rather have, a quarter today or a dollar thirty days from now. If he has a present problem that a quarter will solve, he may think that the quarter today is much more important than a dollar thirty days in the future.

The deception involved in this vanishing point idea has in it a great danger for us. This is the particular deception that got Esau into so much trouble. We recall that day when Esau came home hungry. He was far enough away from food that his will to resist the hunger was close to the vanishing point. Esau's brother Jacob said to him, "Esau, if you will assign over to me your birthright (that is, if you will give me title to all of your cattle, your land, your barns, and your goods), I will give you a mess of pottage."

To a man who had just had a good dinner, that kind of a proposition would not sound very attractive, but Esau was hungry, and I suppose that he might have thought, "What good will all of this wealth and land do me in ten years from now? I am hungry, and I want something to eat right now." His hunger changed Esau's perspective. His birthright looked as if it was quite a long way down the road, and it then seemed to him to be of very little consequence.

74

Therefore, Esau traded off his birthright for a mess of pottage. (See Genesis 25:29-34.)

Most of us make similar kinds of mistakes every day. Because of deception of perspective, we trade off some future birthright for a present pottage. It might help us to live more constructively if we really understood that the tapering-off process always has a vanishing point at its end. Understanding this ought to make it easier for us to protect ourselves against its dangers. Unless we learn how to make some compensations for the deception, we can get ourselves into some very serious difficulties. Deception in our perspective can quickly cheat us out of an education, a character, our material prosperity, our happiness, and every other one of God's blessings.

We remember the old legend of Faust, who made a deal that if Satan would serve him for twenty-four years, punishing Faust's enemies, aiding his friends, and helping him to have a good time, then Faust would forever deliver up his soul to Satan. To Faust this may have seemed like a great idea. Twenty-four years was a long time, and whatever happened beyond that time seemed to be very unimportant. Accordingly, the twenty-four years began and Faust had many wonderful experiences. But almost before he was aware of it he was told, "Thine hour is come." This was the first time that Faust had ever thought about the reckoning. Then he said to himself, "Ah, Faustus, thou hast now but one bare hour to live and then thou must be damned eternally."

For the first time Faust knew that he had cheated himself and he wanted to change the situation, but it was too late. Then he prayed and said, "Oh, God, if thou canst have no mercy on my soul, at least grant some end to my incessant pain. Let Faustus live in hell a thousand years, or even a hundred thousand, but at last be saved." He knew, however, that according to his bargain, even this could never be. He sat and watched the clock tick off the seconds and finally, just before the hour struck, the last words of Faust before he died were: "Faustus is gone to hell." Faust had been robbed of his eternal life by a deception in his own perspective. And this problem is one that we should all be concerned about.

Someone has said that heaven is all right—it is just too far away. But there are ways in which we may bring heaven closer. There are also ways in which we may stay near to God. Certainly we can greatly enrich our own lives when we learn to fully understand that the road does not get narrower, and that it actually does continue beyond the point where it vanishes from our view. In fact, the most important parts of our entire existence, both in this life and in the life to come, lie beyond the place that we now identify as the vanishing point.

One of the most important laws of success is the law of exercise, which is the process by which we get growth and an enlargement of our abilities. However, if the muscles become inactive, they immediately begin decreasing in strength and finally disappear. In both size and strength, all progress soon reaches its vanishing point if inactivity is imposed. Even faith, integrity, morality, love, and intelligence have vanishing points if we permit this deadly tapering-off process. When one starts taking too many liberties with the truth, his integrity begins a steady decline and eventually disappears. When a person makes enough exceptions to righteousness, then the rails of right and wrong seem to get so close together that he is unable to tell which is one and which is the other.

Some people get themselves so involved with sex perversions and other evils that even the finest morality may soon reach its vanishing point. Just as a stone that slips from the fingers will always fall to the ground, so will a standard of value that slips from the moral grasp also fall. After a period of evil indulgence, some people say about truth, or morality, or patriotism, "I couldn't care less." Their concern itself has reached its vanishing point. To keep our faith strong, we must constantly exercise it. Even procrastination or the postponement of an activity can cause fatal deterioration in which one no longer believes or cares or practices.

Our forefathers used a phrase "the great beyond." This might help us to understand the great truth that much of the most important part of our lives took place before we were born and will come after we die, just as most of the facts of our universe lie beyond the sunrises and sunsets of our understanding.

We must be very careful that our faith is not allowed to die and disappear before we arrive at that great destination which is our natural birthright and destiny. May God help us to stay close to him so that we may develop eyes that see and ears that hear and hearts that understand. Then with the telescopes of faith and righteousness we may reach the great goals that God has ordained.

16
The Tradition of the Holy Grail

The life of Christ is the most constructive influence available for our lives. In his antemortal estate he was associated with his Eternal Father, Elohim, in the presidency of heaven. It was through him that our earth was created. As Jehovah, he led the forces of heaven against the rebellion of Lucifer, and it was under his leadership that Lucifer was cast out of heaven.

In the meridian of time he came into our world and redeemed us from death. He atoned for our individual sins, and upon the cross he gave his life for us.

On the last Thursday night of his mortal life, just before the arrest leading to his crucifixion on Friday morning, he ate his last supper with the twelve apostles and instituted the sacrament. About this event the scripture says:

"And as they were eating, Jesus took bread, and blessed it, and brake it, and gave it to the disciples, and said, Take, eat; this is my body.

"And he took the cup, and gave thanks, and gave it to them, saying, Drink ye all of it;

"For this is my blood of the new testament, which is shed for many for the remission of sins." (Matthew 26: 26-28.)

Jesus said we must do this always, in remembrance of him. By remembering him in the spirit of his service to us, we are more likely to make of our lives what he intended.

There is an interesting ancient tradition about this holy sacrament. An ancient tradition, growing out of what happened at the Last Supper, was referred to by James Russell Lowell in 1848 as a basis for his great narrative poem "The Vision of Sir Launfal." The tradition is to the effect that the cup out of which Jesus drank at the last supper became the property of Joseph of Arimathea. Joseph was not

78

only a follower of Jesus, but he was also his uncle. It was Joseph who went to Pilate and asked for the body of Jesus. It was Joseph who took the body of Christ down from the cross and laid it in his own tomb. And it was in Joseph's tomb that the resurrection of Jesus took place.

Joseph was engaged in the tin business and had large interests in England, where he spent much of his time, and tradition has it that this cup or chalice or grail out of which Jesus drank was taken by Joseph to England, where it remained for many years in the custody of some of Joseph's descendants.

The cup became the object of many pilgrimages and much adoration from the people. It was incumbent upon those who were the custodians of the Holy Grail to keep themselves spotlessly chaste in thought, word, and deed. Because one of the keepers failed in this important requirement, the Holy Grail disappeared. Naturally this was a great disappointment to the people of England, and the resulting concern caused many important individuals to take up the search in order to find it and bring its blessings back to the people.

Inasmuch as this sacred vessel could be retained only be someone living the purest kind of life, it naturally followed that it would bring the highest personal honor to the one who was able to recover it. At that time some of those considered to be the best men in England were members of King Arthur's court. These knights had dedicated their lives and themselves to acts of charity and deeds of righteousness. Finally the great Sir Launfal, the chief of King Arthur's men, decided to personally take up the search. In so doing he made a solemn vow that he would never stop searching for the Holy Grail until it was found. He also vowed that in every detail he would live the kind of life that would be sure to win the Lord's favor.

Just before he set out on his journey he had a dream in which in the night he spent his entire lifetime living an ideal life while searching for the Holy Grail. In this lifetime of his dream, he experienced all the privations and sufferings that would naturally be connected with such a search. However, he was unsuccessful, and years later, when he was old and after all his material wealth had been exhausted, he returned to the area that had once been his home. It was Christmas time, and the weather was bitter cold. As he was thinking of his life and experiences, he was approached by a leprous beggar asking for alms. Sir Launfal loved all men, and doing good was the purpose of his life. He had almost nothing of a material nature to give the beggar, but he had a great spirit of brotherhood and love, the spirit of Christ, whom he served. As a token of brotherhood, he divided with the leper his last crust of bread; and, with his wooden bowl, he dipped water from the frozen streamlet nearby and gave the beggar a drink.

Then the most thrilling experience in Sir Launfal's life took place. The leper was transfigured before him, and Sir Launfal saw not only the Holy Grail but the Savior himself. His own wooden cup became the holy vessel out of which the Lord shared the sacrament with Sir Launfal himself. Mr. Lowell described the beauty of this great experience. He said:

> The heart within him was ashes and dust;
> He parted in twain his single crust,
> He broke the ice on the streamlet's brink,
> And gave the leper to eat and drink,
> 'Twas a mouldy crust of coarse brown bread,
> 'Twas water out of a wooden bowl,—
> Yet with fine wheaten bread was the leper fed,
> And 'twas red wine he drank with his thirsty soul.
>
> As Sir Launfal mused with a downcast face,
> A light shone round about the place.
> The leper no longer crouched at his side,
> But stood before him glorified,
> Shining and tall and fair and straight
> As the pillar that stood by the Beautiful Gate,—
> Himself the Gate whereby men can
> Enter the temple of God in Man.
>
> His words were shed softer than leaves from the pine,
> And they fell on Sir Launfal as snows on the brine,
> That mingle their softness and quiet in one
> With a shaggy unrest they float down upon;
> And a voice that was softer than silence said,
> "Lo, it is I, be not afraid!

In many climes, without avail,
Thou hast spent thy life for the holy grail;
Behold, it is here,—this cup which thou
Didst fill at the streamlet for me but now;
This crust is my body broken for thee;
This water his blood who died on the tree;
This Holy Supper is kept, indeed,
In whatso we share with another's need;
Not what we give, but what we share,
For the gift without the giver is bare;
Who gives himself with his alms feeds three,
Himself, his hungering neighbor, and me."

Sir Launfal woke as from a swound:
"The grail in my castle here is found!
Hang my idle armor up on the wall,
Let it be the spider's banquet-hall.
He must be fenced with stronger mail
Who would seek and find the Holy Grail."

This may be only a beautiful story and yet it is much more than that, for it teaches the great virtues of righteousness, love, and devotion to God. It teaches the great lesson that it was not merely the cup that the Savior touched that was important. The sacrament was the token of a covenant of a lifetime of obedience and righteousness. Because of the way Sir Launfal had lived and the service he had given, he had made his own life such that he could personally identify with the Lord himself. And maybe we ought to learn something from this important idea.

The blessings of life are just as important to us as they ever were to Sir Launfal or to Peter or to anyone else. How much time and dedication should we be willing to expend in a search for godliness and eternal life? If we always remember our greatest benefactor in the right spirit, we will be a different kind of people than if we devote our thoughts and ourselves to lesser things. The Savior left no possible doubt about the fact that to properly partake of the sacrament is very important, and certainly it is just as important now as it was in the days of Joseph of Arimathea or in the days of James Russell Lowell. Jesus gave the sacrament for our benefit to help us to remember him when he was no longer with us personally.

81

Since the days of Jesus, not only has the sacramental chalice been lost, but after the crucifixion the apostles also suffered violent deaths, and many of Christ's doctrines were lost because of apostasy. However, after the long night of the spiritual dark ages, the gospel has again been restored to the earth. On the day of the organization of the Church of Christ in these last days, the sacrament of the Lord's supper was reinstituted, and the exact words of the prayer for both the bread and the water were given by direct revelation. The Lord has said:

"It is expedient that the church meet together often to partake of the bread and wine in remembrance of the Lord Jesus;

"And the elder or priest shall administer it; and after this manner shall he administer it—he shall kneel with the church and call upon the Father in solemn prayer, saying:

"O God, the Eternal Father, we ask thee in the name of thy Son, Jesus Christ, to bless and sanctify this bread to the souls of all those who partake of it, that they may eat in remembrance of the body of thy Son, and witness unto thee, O God, the Eternal Father, that they are willing to take upon them the name of thy Son, and always remember him and keep his commandments which he has given them; that they may always have his Spirit to be with them. Amen." (D&C 20:75-77.)

What a beautiful prayer! What a beautiful covenant! And what a wonderful opportunity it affords us to remember the Savior and live those holy covenants that he desires to guide our lives.

Jesus said, "This do ye always in remembrance of me." Certainly Sir Launfal would not have been eligible for the great favor of the Lord if he had not been interested in keeping the commandments. Or how would we classify ourselves if the emblems of his sacrifice were being administered by his authority, but we were not interested enough even to put in an appearance? Sir Launfal was willing to spend his entire life in the hope of bringing back to the people of England the blessings of the sacramental cup. Even more important, the Lord himself has now made a full and complete restoration of the entire sacrament service itself. How discouraging it must be to him when we continue in our sins, and there are even many members of the restored church who do not attend their sacrament meeting.

We have been given the power to greatly enrich ourselves through having the spirit and the covenants and the blessings of the sacrament in our lives. The Lord wants every one of us to belong to his church, and he wants everyone to attend sacrament meeting. If we all have the proper spirit of reverence, order, faith, obedience, and service, the holy supper may be kept indeed so that all of the blessings of the gosepl may be continually had in our midst. Certainly we have this in common with the tradition: we must keep ourselves worthy of our promised blessings. May we always remember him and keep his commandments, that we may always have his Spirit to be with us.

*"If you cannot keep my commandments
you cannot be saved in the kingdom of
my Father."
(D&C 18:46.)*

Overcoming
Evil

17
A Wasted Probation

God has appointed unto us this earth life as a period of our mortal probation. He has not only ordained life and birth and experience for us, but he has also given us death. He himself has said: "And thus did I, the Lord God, appoint unto man the days of his probation—that by his natural death he might be raised in immortality unto eternal life, even as many as would believe." (D&C 29:43.)

What a tremendous gift this great opportunity of life is! President Joseph Fielding Smith has said that mortality is the most important part of eternity. All of us have passed the requirements of our first estate with flying colors. Now all that stands between us and an eternal, glorified life in God's presence is what we do in these few remaining years of mortality. If we are faithful to his commands, then we may become like our eternal heavenly parents.

A probation is a proceeding designed to ascertain truth, to form character, and to develop other important qualifications. It is a period of trial, a time of testing, a time of probing. It is an opportunity for developing our abilities and proving our virtues. If we could calculate the value of our mortal probation, we might be motivated to make the most out of it.

In our first estate, we walked by sight. In our second estate, we are supposed to learn to walk a little way by faith. Here we are "added upon" with mortal bodies, without which we could never have a fulness of joy. Here for the first time we have that miraculous power of procreation, by which it is possible for us to create children in God's own image, organize families, and have them eternally sealed together by the power of the priesthood.

When we earned the privilege of being born, we opened the door for our greatest opportunity, but we also assumed the tremendous responsibilities that go with it. We were not created sinners or weaklings or failures, but mortals. And

God will hold us responsible for the choices that we make here. We have been equipped with instinctive knowledge of good and evil, besides the whisperings of the Spirit.

This life is made up of the greatest of all experiences. Those who sin will be given an opportunity to repent and cleanse themselves. Sometimes persons who commit offenses against the state are not imprisoned, but are put on probation. That is, they are released under suspended sentences and put under supervision with specific conditions imposed. It is the usual custom that the person who is on probation must report to the court or one of its officers at stated intervals. It is a very serious matter when one violates his probation. And the greatest opportunity of our lives is to use the period of our mortal probation to build strength, beauty, and character into our lives.

Alma, a pre-Columbus American prophet, said: ". . . there was a space granted unto man in which he might repent; therefore this life became a probationary state; a time to prepare to meet God; a time to prepare for that endless state which . . . is after the resurrection of the dead." (Alma 12:24.)

In one of the great sermons of the world, the Nephite prophet Jacob said:

"And [God] commandeth all men that they must repent, and be baptized in his name, having perfect faith in the Holy One of Israel, or they cannot be saved in the kingdom of God.

"And if they will not repent and believe in his name, and be baptized in his name, and endure to the end, they must be damned; for the Lord God, the Holy One of Israel, has spoken it.

"Wherefore he has given a law; and where there is no law given there is not punishment; and where there is no punishment there is no condemnation; and where there is no condemnation the mercies of the Holy One of Israel have claim upon them, because of the atonement; for they are delivered by the power of him.

"For the atonement satisfieth the demands of his justice upon all those who have not the law given to them, that they are delivered from that awful monster, death and hell, and the devil, and the lake of fire and brimstone, which is endless torment; and they are restored to that God who gave them breath, which is the Holy One of Israel.

"But wo unto him that has the law given; yea, that has all the commandments of God, like unto us, and that transgresseth them, and that wasteth the days of his probation, for awful is his state!" (2 Nephi 9:23-27.)

It is a little difficult for anyone to imagine anything quite as unpleasant and as unprofitable as to waste this short and very important period of our mortality. The prophet said, ". . . wo unto all those who die in their sins, for they shall return to God, and behold his face, and remain in their sins." (2 Nephi 9:38.)

What a thrill it ought to be to every human being in the world to be alive! What a joy to know about our destiny and feel within ourselves that we are children of God, with incomparable opportunities for real self-fulfillment!

Think how much worse it might be in eternity for those who have wasted the days of their probation. The scriptures make it clear that there is an everlasting place of intense mental and physical suffering for those who seriously violate their mortal probation.

All principles and ordinances of the gospel have to do with the celestial kingdom. If we are only interested in the lower orders of life, then we don't need to be baptized. We don't need to pay our tithing. We don't need to be married in the temple. But on the other hand, what would it be like to be without the joys of having a loving family? Some people can understand what it is like here to have nothing to do, no one to love, and little to hope for. That must not happen to us hereafter.

One of the fundamental laws of life is that all development is self-development, and what a challenge is placed before us to make the most of our probation while the opportunity is available! We can make ourselves into the most magnificent of all creations if we follow the directions that God has already given us. May he abundantly bless our efforts!

18
Sins Against the Personality

The biggest problems of our world are caused by sin. Sin involves disobedience to God. The apostle John says, ". . . sin is the transgression of the law." (1 John 3:4.) Transgression is a subject that we need to know a lot more about, because before we can solve any problem, we need to understand it and know in detail what causes it.

The history of our world presents a rather dismal spectacle of wrongdoing. Our present age is characterized by crime, delinquencies, rebellions, and atheism. As a result of our transgressions, our jails are full, our reform schools and mental institutions are bulging with inmates, and our divorce courts are crowded. We sin against God. We transgress the laws of the land. We commit sins against property. Many people wantonly destroy beauty, peace, and happiness without any hope of securing any advantages for themselves thereby. Many religious leaders have apostatized from God and are teaching for doctrines the commands of men, which have a form of godliness but deny the power thereof.

Standing close to those sins that we commit against God are such sins as ignorance, idleness, indifference, inferiority, and guilt, which we launch against ourselves. And one of the most serious of all of these sins is the sin against the personality.

Personality is that tremendous set of qualities that make us people. These are those wonderful traits to which God has given us an exclusive right and which set us apart from all of God's other creations. We are not superior to machines in power. In some cases plants and animals have greater abilities and many have more accurate instincts than men do. But in the gifts of personality, God is man's only fellow in the universe. No plant or animal has ever been given the ability to smile or to worship or to make choices—in short, to be a person.

A young woman was once asked what those privileges in life were that she appreciated more than any other. She said, "More than anything else I want to be myself." She wanted to be able to think, make decisions, meditate, laugh, love, sing, grow, and enjoy. She wanted to be a sovereign soul and someday be like God.

Our most serious sins against ourselves come when we destroy in us God's image in which we ourselves were made, or we allow the lines of our identity to become corroded or indistinct by the corrosion or attrition of sin. Every human being is distinct. We are not supposed to be someone else. And when we destroy those great human qualities in others by exercising unrighteous dominion over them or making them less than they are, we tend to make human beings into something that may more closely resemble animals or things than people.

A modern-day scripture points out this weakness in our nature when it says:

"We have learned by sad experience that it is the nature and disposition of almost all men, as soon as they get a little authority, as they suppose, they will immediately begin to exercise unrighteous dominion."

This great revelation goes on to say that:

"No power or influence can or ought to be maintained by virtue of the priesthood, only by persuasion, by long-suffering, by gentleness and meekness, and by love unfeigned;

"By kindness, and pure knowledge, which shall greatly enlarge the soul without hypocrisy, and without guile—

"Reproving betimes with sharpness, when moved upon by the Holy Ghost; and then showing forth afterwards an increased love toward him whom thou hast reproved, lest he esteem thee to be his enemy;

"That he may know that thy faithfulness is stronger than the cords of death.

"Let thy bowels also be full of charity towards all men, and to the household of faith, and let virtue garnish thy thoughts unceasingly; then shall thy confidence wax strong in the presence of God; and the doctrine of the priesthood shall distil upon thy soul as the dews from heaven.

"The Holy Ghost shall be thy constant companion, and thy scepter an unchanging scepter of righteousness and truth; and thy dominion shall be an everlasting dominion, and without compulsory means it shall flow unto thee forever and ever." (D&C 121:39-46.)

That is a public relations statement of the highest quality. However, we don't always follow it. One of the worst places for its abuse is in the marriage relationship. Mental cruelty in marriage is much more than just an idle phrase. We might paraphrase Shakespeare to say, He who steals my purse steals trash, but he who makes me less than I am or deprives me of the joy of living robs me of that which never enriches him but makes me poor indeed.

A woman recently filed suit for divorce. All of her early life she had looked forward to the time when she would have this important experience of being married and having a family. She had dreamed of the knight in shining armor who would someday come riding by to carry her away to their own castle on the mountaintop. Stated another way, she expected to marry a man—God's greatest creation who had been formed in God's likeness and endowed with godly attributes and potentialities. He would be fully worthy to take her to the temple of the Lord, where the proper foundations of a family would be laid so that it would last for time and for eternity. They each would make and live eternal covenants and pledges of love, loyalty, fidelity, industry, and responsibility. Their family would be blessed with children who would be taught by precept and example to walk in the ways of the Lord.

The natural consequence of such a righteous association would be eternal glory, eternal happiness, endless progression, and eternal increase. This young woman entered into marriage with the highest expectations, feeling that both of them would do exactly as they should. But sometimes love is blind, and she was sadly disappointed. The man she married turned out to be very lazy, sloppy in his dress and person, and extremely egotistical. He interpreted his role as head of the house as some kind of a matrimonial dictatorship. He expected that his wife should accept his every word as law, whether he was right or wrong. He kept reminding her that he had more education than she had. He let it be known that he felt that she was extremely fortunate to have him as her husband.

At first she felt that this must be some kind of temporary insanity from which he would recover. She thought it would be impossible for one human being to continue to make a fellow human being so miserable, especially when that other human being was his soul's companion. But instead of the leopard losing his spots, the spots kept getting larger. His disease of unrighteous dominion was increasing to epidemic proportions. Some subconscious sense of inferiority seemed to demand that he humiliate her and make her beg and plead. Actually he was destroying those wonderful God-given qualities of personality and was making her into a thing instead of a person. We have police forces to prevent crime. Governments regulate business. But in her marriage there was no hand to stay his unrighteous dominion. And when one discovers that those qualities, feelings, and opinions that make one a person have been destroyed, then there is not much left.

This is not an isolated case, for as pointed out in the revelation, the sin of unrighteous dominion produces one of the major problems of our day, and it shows itself particularly devastating in our present destructive epidemic of divorce.

One wife recently reported that her husband had not had a job for ten years because he could not get along with those with whom he worked. He required her to turn all of her money over to him, and he acted as the boss in all of the details of the lives of members of his family.

You say, "This man is sick," and so he is. But everyone is sick who lies and cheats and who is immoral, lazy, and unfair. In some degree the sickness of unrighteous dominion gets into far too many lives. The revelation says that "it is the nature and disposition of almost all men, as soon as they get a little authority, as they suppose, they will immediately begin to exercise unrighteous dominion." It is by this

94

process that we tear people down and make them into things.

By way of contrast, what a great idea it is, both in and out of marriage, to build people up, to encourage them to have opinions, convictions, standards, and ideas—to let one's family have a significant voice in family management and take an important part in family activities. They may make some mistakes, but the mistakes will not be as great in a family democracy as in a dictatorship. And how is one ever going to learn in a dictatorship in which he is not permitted to have some ideas of his own? Certainly no husband is intelligent enough to dictate in all areas of family life; every wife ought to have some say in doing her own thing in those fields where she is most qualified.

Next in importance to the human spirit and the human body is the human personality. Even a human body or a human spirit without a personality would be of little value. What a thrilling idea that in the design of God you will be yourself and I will be myself throughout eternity, with quickened senses, amplified powers of perception, and vastly increased capacity for love, harmony, fairness, understanding, and happiness. The greatest of all of our human concepts is the immortality of the personality and the endless glory of the human soul.

19
The Other Side of the *But*

I recently read an interesting book written by Marcus Bach entitled *The World of Serendipity*. Mr. Bach makes some challenging applications of an idea made famous many years ago by Horace Walpole in his story of the three princes of Serendip. Serendip was a part of the ancient kingdom of Ceylon, and in their travels the three princes were always finding important things for which they were not directly searching. As a result of this story, a new word came into existence, called "serendipity," which means that many of the most worthwhile things of life come through a kind of indirection.

An example of how serendipity works may be found in the experience of Columbus, who started out to find the East Indies and discovered America instead.

Sir Alexander Fleming, the discoverer of penicillin, spoke of "serendipity in science." He pointed out that most of the wonder drugs, including penicillin, were discovered while the discoverer was looking for something else. The discoverer of the antitoxin for smallpox was a milkmaid who had cowpox.

Happiness is another example; it is in large measure a kind of by-product and is seldom obtained by direct pursuit. The sweetest friendships are usually those that are not deliberately courted, but rather the ones that come as a result of something else. Often when we woo a thing too conscientiously or make our attack too direct, we seem to frighten it so that it escapes us.

It is interesting that one of the best ways to rest is to practice serendipity. That is, one of the best ways to rest is to work harder and more effectively. Therefore, when you want rest, strive for greater accomplishment. Someone once remarked to Abraham Lincoln that he looked tired and that he should take things a little easier. He replied that it was his heart that was tired, and in order to rest his heart, he must go on at an accelerated pace. A job is always the hardest when we work at it the easiest, and the easiest when we work at it the hardest. An automobile uses much more gasoline per mile when running at four miles per hour than when running at forty miles per hour. When we are ahead of our job we love it; when our job is ahead of us we hate it. No one ever quits while he is ahead. No one ever gets tired while he is winning.

Each of us often does things that prevent us from reaching the most worthwhile objectives. For example, an author tells a story of his Aunt Selma, who had an interesting infirmity he calls "but-a-phobia." She was always on the wrong side of the *but*. Sometimes even when speaking about the things that she thought were the best, she would usually then launch into a long post-lamentation about what was wrong with them. Once after she returned from a sale at a store she said, "It was all right, *but* the bargains were gone." Again she said, "The movie was good, *but* it should have had a different ending." "The church service was not too bad, *but* the hymns didn't fit the sermon."

But-a-phobia may be all right if one stays on the right side of the *but*. However, if one gets on the wrong side of the *but,* he often tends to be negative, disloyal, disorderly, and atheistic. *But*-a-phobia is a common complaint. One variety of *but*-a-phobia makes many young people rebel against their parents and run away from home. It is the *but*-ers who are always trying to tear down the establishment.

Jesus was talking about a sort of *but*-a-phobia when he said that there were some people who had eyes that couldn't see and ears that couldn't hear and hearts that failed to understand. (See Matthew 13:15.) What happens is that we don't see the right things and we put the emphasis in the wrong places. We see the molehills and miss the mountains. We quickly pass over the good so we can emphasize the bad. We hear the evil, but we can't hear the inspiring, the patriotic, and the uplifting. We think we see some advantages in dishonesty, immorality, and the various forms of evil while we fail to recognize the advantages of honor, loyalty, and righteousness. We say we are poor *but* honest. We don't obey the law *but* we do pay our debts.

I once heard three men being discussed for employment. Of one it was said, "He knows his business and he is strictly honest, *but* he is lazy." Of the second it was said, "He is a hard worker, *but* he is dishonest." Of the third it was said, "He is a fine gentleman with a good personality, *but* he has poor judgment." I discovered that no matter what may go before, we had better pay strict attention when we come to the *but*.

In the story referred to earlier, Aunt Selma finally got around the other side of the *but*. No one ever really discovered why she made the change. She merely said that she "just got to thinking." A lot of important things happen when people actually get down to thinking. When Aunt Selma got around to the other side of the *but,* life became a lot more interesting. Then when she went to an unprofitable sale she would say, "All the bargains were gone, *but* it was a lot of fun just the same." "The movie should have had a different ending, *but* it was a very educational movie." "The church songs didn't fit, *but* I got a lot of good out of the sermon."

As we journey through life, we always find a lot of so-called chance and coincidence. We run into a lot of unexpected events that are a part of the natural order of things, and it is important that we make the most of the good and the least of the bad. We should be impressed with the truth that our personalities are shaped by our points of view, and we can have a good point of view about every experience, and many so-called accidental happenings can be made purposeful.

When one reverses his point of view, he starts his life anew. A small change in attitudes and activities can make a great difference in the result. One might say, "It is good to be alive, but we cannot live forever." However, it is much better to say, "We cannot live forever, but it is good to be alive." The first *but* implies fatalism; the second gives a hint of a sense of radiant hope. The first affirms and then denies; the second erases the denial with an affirmation. Consider Emerson's famous saying, "Say not, 'Behold an hour of my life is gone,' but rather say, 'I have lived an hour.'"

To say "I would like to be successful, but . . ." has often plunged people into moods of indecision and despair. It is behind the *but* that we put all of our alibis, rationalizations, and procrastinations. So many negative, discouraging, belittling things that follow our *buts* can neutralize the finest objectives that went before them. "I know I have ability, but I was born on the wrong side of the railroad tracks." "I know I should go to church, but my parents took me too much when I was young." "I would like to be a good member of the church, but there are too many hypocrites there."

If one sees obstacles in his opportunities, he is a pessimist. If he sees opportunities in his obstacles, he is an optimist. It is also interesting that "U" is at the center of every B-U-T—and the other side of the BUT can be the other side of "U."

Is it possible that the *but* in most of our problems and challenges may be the axis upon which our decisions can most successfully be made to turn? It is perhaps at this point that we may recognize our greatest strengths and learn to master our deepest weaknesses.

What a great joy to stand out against wrong! A great man who was once a candidate for president of the United States said, "I'd rather be right than be president." Even suffering can be made pleasant if one is on the right side of the *but*. One great woman has been paralyzed from her waist down for most of her life. Someone once said to her, "My, how suffering does color life." This woman replied, "That is so, but I myself intend to select the colors." She didn't say, "I would have been happy and useful but I am paralyzed." What a thrill that each of us can be the master of his own destiny!

Like Aunt Selma, most of us need to start doing some thinking. We might think of a *but* as a fence, and if things are going against us, it may be that we are on the wrong side of the fence. Some of our *buts* need to be entirely removed, while we merely need to get on the other side of some others. There are a lot of sins, weaknesses, and evils that we need to get rid of, and there are a lot of attitudes, issues, and habits that we need to get on the other side of.

Too often we affirm and then deny instead of erasing all denial with a strong affirmation. If we can do this, then we can say with the poet:

> Night swoops on me with blackest wings,
> But I'll succeed.
> I see the stars that darkness brings,
> And I'll succeed.
> No force on earth can make me cower
> Because each moment and each hour,
> I still affirm with strength and power,
> I shall succeed.

May we always be found on the right side of the *but*!

20
The Tares

Jesus used many parables in his teaching. He made constructive comparisons in his formal teachings as well as in his ordinary conversation. He explained in images that his listeners understood concepts that are more difficult to understand. To fully understand a thing, we usually need to see it from several points of view. We ought to know the good and the bad in every situation. We need to understand the obstacles as well as the opportunities.

In the thirteenth chapter of Matthew, Jesus compared the kingdom of heaven with a field of wheat in which an enemy had planted tares. In those days a tare was a weed capable of vigorous growth, and when it was young it closely resembled the young wheat. The Savior said:

"The kingdom of heaven is likened unto a man which sowed good seeds in his field;

"But while men slept, his enemy came and sowed tares among the wheat, and went his way.

"But when the blade was sprung up, and brought forth fruit, then appeared the tares also.

"So the servants of the householder came and said unto him, Sir, didst not thou sow good seed in thy field? from whence then hath it tares?

"He said unto them, An enemy hath done this. The servants said unto him, Wilt thou then that we go and gather them up?

"But he said, Nay; lest while ye gather up the tares, ye root up also the wheat with them.

"Let both grow together until the harvest: and in the time of harvest I will say to the reapers, Gather ye together first the tares, and bind them in bundles to burn them: but gather the wheat into my barn." (Matthew 13:24-30.)

In this parable Jesus was not trying to tell people how to improve their wheat production. He was trying to help them improve their human experience. The tares he had in mind were the weeds that grow so prolifically in human lives.

In analyzing this parable, we can see several problems inherent in the situation. If the laborers should go into the field and pull up the tares while the plants were young, much of the wheat would be either uprooted or trampled down, so that a virtual crop failure would be the consequence. The alternative also has some problems. Tares are always very much more vigorous than wheat, and they always get most of their nourishment out of the soil. If they are pulled out early, the wheat crop is not so seriously damaged, but if they are allowed to grow with the wheat, the grain yield might be cut in half. And that still doesn't describe all of the problems. At the time of the harvest a lot of extra workers will be needed to sort out, tie, and burn the tares, so the yield will not only be cut in half, but the labor costs will also be doubled.

This parable is particularly timely, because the enemy has never been as active in sowing tare seeds as now, and the tares have never been more vigorous. Just think how much strength is being sucked from our lives by the tares of ignorance, the tares of sin, the tares of crime, the tares of sloth, and the tares of weakness. If we let them grow until the harvest time, it will be pretty difficult to ever get them out, and in the meantime, we will be crowded and cramped, resulting in scrubby wheat. Someone has suggested how much better off we would be if we applied a third alternative and sprayed the tares with some good weed killer just as they are getting started. Then all of the fertility, sunshine, and rain would be available to mature the wheat of our lives.

Atheism is a tare that should be dealt with early. Immorality is a tare. Dishonesty is a tare. Drug, alcohol, and nicotine addictions are all vigorous, fast-growing, fertility-consuming tares. One modern-day tare that is particularly destructive is a multipurpose weed called irresponsibility.

On the other hand, no trait could be more valuable or beautiful than that quality of always being fully responsible.

Some of the synonyms for responsibility are reliability, imperturbability, respectability, trustworthiness. A human being who is responsible is a joy to everyone. How pleasant to be associated with one who can always be depended upon, who always pays his own way, who always holds himself fully accountable to himself and to God.

On that night during the Revolutionary War when Benedict Arnold tried to sell West Point to the British, no one knew how far the treason had gone. General George Washington needed someone to stand guard for the rest of the night, someone whose character was completely above suspicion. In choosing the father of Daniel Webster for the assignment he said, "Captain Webster, I can trust you."

It has been said that to be trusted is a greater compliment than to be loved. We hear one of the most exciting phrases in our language when some capable human being says, "I'll be responsible." By comparison, how miserable are those tares that make one unpredictable, irresponsible, unstable, unthoughtful, unthankful, and unholy.

A mother was recently telling about her nineteen-year-old son who is tampering with dope. He will tell any lie even to his mother to get what he wants. His word means absolutely nothing. His promises can never be depended upon. The fact that he is breaking his mother's heart doesn't seem to make the slightest impression on him. The only things that he can understand are his own selfish appetites and passions.

Someone once said that you should never criticize a man for what he does while he is drunk, because he is then not responsible. But even a drunkard makes his worst decisions while he is perfectly sober, for that is when he decides to get drunk.

When people get married, they make certain covenants that are binding before God, society, and each other. Then sometimes while they sleep, the enemy comes and sows tares among the wheat, and if the tares are allowed to grow, the wheat is soon so crowded out that the marriage fails. The finest marriage safeguard is for each spouse to pull up the first ugly little tare that pokes up its head among their wheat.

Recently I received a letter from a young husband seeking someone to try to persuade his wife to continue to live with him. They had been married for three years and already his wheat field was a solid mass of tares. He had come from a good home and had a fine religious background, but the crowding of the tares had caused him to make almost every mistake.

His wife persuaded him to get some marriage counseling, but because he continued to let his tares grow, she finally filed for divorce. Even so, he imagines that he can solve his problems by writing a letter to a complete stranger who lives only a few miles away and that the most important problem of his life can be solved by mail without his even going to discuss the problem in person.

Several times in his letter he repeated his assertion that he loves his wife very much, and always has done. He feels that she is a wonderful person. She gave up her own education and got a job and sent him through college. "But," he said, "I fell in with the wrong people and began drinking, staying away from home nights, and refusing to tell my wife where I was. I even began to doubt the value of religion and morality. During the second year of our marriage, my wife left me twice. When she finally filed for divorce I went to see her father and promised him I would straighten up my life and become a more responsible husband. He persuaded her to come back to me, but I was still trying to cover up my sins instead of correcting them, and I continued to lie to her a great deal. All of this time a deep distrust and a deep dislike for me has been growing up in her.

"My resolutions to repent and make amends usually last for only a few weeks and then I gradually go back to my old friends and my old ways. My wife put up with this until my graduation in June, when she again filed for divorce. She had been hurt and abused to the point that she feels no love, respect, or trust for me at all."

This young man wanted someone to persuade his wife to come back to him. But his wife could see only a field full of tares, and she believed that she had made about as many hopeless contributions to him as she could afford. She didn't dare to have a family of her own until she had a husband who showed a few signs of manhood. She had already wasted three precious years of her own life. She had given up her own education and had lost real opportunities for a happy marriage. She felt that the tares of immaturity, irresponsibility, lack of manhood, and lack of basic character were so firmly established in his life that building anything worthwhile into him would be too difficult. She remembered the old proverb saying that rotten wood cannot be carved. She didn't want to spend her life trying to make a silk purse out of a sow's ear.

If this young man really wanted to change, anyone could tell him how to solve his problems. But he can't follow even the very finest directions, because he is irresponsible. Irresponsibility makes it difficult for him to even help himself. He doesn't know how to keep sacred promises or have enough basic honor to cover the agreement he made with her father.

What a tragedy to be irresponsbile! God can resurrect a dead body, but who can resurrect a dead faith or revive a destroyed love or wipe out the devastating effects of irresponsibility as long as the irresponsible one insists on growing tares with the wheat?

Many people seem willing to keep on paying the penalties of irresponsibility instead of cleaning out the tares that caused it. Someone said that the best way to break a bad habit is to drop it, and one of the finest resolves that anyone can make is to be responsible.

No matter how successful our deceits may be, tares will continue to suck the vitality out of our lives. There can be no possible peaceful co-existence for wheat and tares. The apostle Paul said, ". . . for what fellowship hath righteousness with unrighteousness? and what communion hath light with darkness?" (2 Corinthians 6:14.)

May each of us resolve today to rid ourselves of those tares that are choking out righteousness in our lives.

21
Lost

An important word that we use often and in many ways is the word *lost*. It has a variety of meanings, many of which are unpleasant. If we understand its good and bad possibilities, we may more effectively protect our own interests. The dictionary says that the word *lost* means that something has gone out of our possession. It may have to do with something that has been ruined or destroyed, either physically, mentally, morally, spiritually, socially, or financially. The dictionary gives some examples of this word's meaning, such as "a lost ship," "a lost fortune," "a lost limb," "a lost honor," "a lost soul."

We speak of the lost arts as those which have ceased to be known or practiced. *Lost* also describes someone who is bewildered, perplexed, or unable to find his way. A child may be lost in the crowd, an island may be lost in the fog, a person may be lost in sin. Some things get lost when they are no longer visible or remembered. Sometimes we get lost because we become insensible to important things. It is very serious to be lost in hopelessness or to have our judgment obscured by the influence of an evil person or idea. It is not so bad when we get lost in thought or lost in our work. Many valuable things are lost because they are wasted, squandered, or ineffectively employed. It may be disastrous when the battle is lost, or the opportunity is lost, or the benefit is lost. Someone wrote about another common loss when he said:

> Lost—
> Somewhere between sunrise and sunset,
> Two golden hours.
> Each is set with sixty diamond minutes.
> There is no reward offered,
> For they are gone forever.

Sometimes we lose our abilities to learn, and then many benefits may be offered to us without making any worthwhile impression. Sometimes our sensibilities may be hardened beyond all hope of recovery, or we may become lost in shame, or lost in failure, or lost in evil. Sometimes we imagine that everyone is lost except us. A little Indian boy was once asked how he got lost. He said, "I'm not lost, the tepee's lost." A pilot sent out a radio message saying, "We are making wonderful time but we are hopelessly lost."

The dictionary gives some of the synonyms for this little four-letter word, such as overthrown, subverted, forfeited, confused, defiled, abandoned, and irreclaimable. As the opposites of lost, we find such words as found, saved, recovered, innocent, and reformed. For one reason or another we lose far too many of the good things in life. If we don't prevent it, one may lose his money, his reputation, his health, his hopes, his ambition, his interest in life, his opportunities, his abilities, and even his soul. One may lose time and faith. And how tragic when we add up all of these losses and find that our lives themselves have been wasted. Only as we stop each of these little leaks and losses can we save the whole.

In the parable of the prodigal son, the Lord tells about a young man who persuaded his father to give him now that portion of the family inheritance that might sometime fall into his hands. The father did as his prodigal son asked. The son then took the wealth that had been acquired by a father's lifetime of toil and wasted it in riotous living. When his money had been squandered, his friends also disappeared. When he was hungry and alone, the son decided to return home. Here he was enthusiastically received by his father, who in great joy said, "This my son was lost and is found. He was dead and is alive again." (See Luke 15:11-32.)

We are not informed what the future of this young man may have been. We might hope that he had been fully and permanently cured of getting lost, though many prodigals never find themselves, and there is a large group of modern prodigals who deliberately get lost. They get lost from morality, lost from reason, and lost from righteousness. Like the prodigal mentioned by Jesus, some may eventually come to themselves, but most just keep getting lost over and over again.

A recent brochure about the inmates of a state penitentiary indicates that the average prisoner has been arrested eleven times. The state tries to induce them to change to a good life, but as soon as they are released from prison, many of them will immediately again get lost in crime. Released prisoners do not thereafter always obey the law. Reformed alcoholics do not always stay reformed. Repentant sinners do not thereafter always follow the straight and narrow way. It is so easy for some people to continually get lost.

Some people have criticized the older brother of the prodigal son. This brother was upset when he came in from working in the field to find his prodigal brother and his friends eating the fatted calf and making merry at a party celebrating his homecoming. There is a debate that probably will never be settled about how many times a prodigal should be permitted to waste the family fortunes and reputation. Certainly the experience of getting lost from honor and righteousness is reenacted millions of times every year. One of the great tragedies of our present world is that there are so many prodigal sons and so many prodigal daughters who are not only losing their families' fortunes, but also losing their honor, their character, their happiness, and almost every other worthwhile thing in life, including their eternal souls.

I recently visited with a very wonderful family. They had a beautiful home. They had great love for each other. They were all highly intelligent and very happy. Their oldest son had just returned home after serving the Church for two years in the mission field. He had been successful in teaching the principles of the gospel to a substantial number of others, and he came home with the high honors of an assignment well filled.

He had been away from home for two years, but in no sense was he lost. Although he was away from his family, he was always close to them and close to God. He had helped many other people find their way in life, and by his study and devotion he had built greater character, strength, and spiritual qualities into himself. His faith-promoting letters had been a continual source of inspiration and uplift to his younger brothers and sisters. Now he is finishing his schooling, and with an alert mind and a good basic character, he is practically assured of outstanding success and genuine happiness in life in the highest meanings of those terms. This fine young man brings indescribable joy into the hearts of his parents and provides a righteous pattern for his younger brothers and sisters.

Then I thought, what a contrast this family presents to those who have lost themselves. Recently a brokenhearted mother told me about her family experience. She and her husband were not inferior in intellect to the parents in the other family, but they had neglected teaching their children those fundamental principles of character and religion, and as a consequence one of their sons is now serving a twenty-year term among hardened criminals in a state penitentiary.

The members of this family have many other problems. The mother is on the verge of mental collapse. She formerly took such great delight in her children. She is still tied to them by the strong bonds of mother-love which cannot easily be broken, but she now has the awful fear that her children will eventually be lost. Even after her convict son is released, he will probably not want to come home. And how desolate she becomes as she feels the loneliness inflicted upon her by the loss of her family!

During our first estate we lived with God our Father. Then we walked by sight. We were sent to earth for one important reason—that we might learn to walk by faith. We know something about those mansions in heaven that God has already prepared for us, but many potentially wonderful people will get lost and never find the celestial kingdom. When Jesus said, ". . . strait is the gate, and narrow is the way, which leadeth unto life, and few there be that find it" (Matthew 7:14), he was speaking about the celestial kingdom.

Just suppose that it will sometime have to be reported to the faithful members of our family and friends that we have gone beyond the point of no return and can never be expected to come home. Then try to imagine anything that could be worse than to get lost from God.

Recently I talked with a mother whose only child had been born out of wedlock. She had summoned this little human being from the world of spirits, and by the creative gifts she had received from God, she had formed him in God's image. When her baby was born, she gave him away to be adopted by people who will always remain completely unknown to her. During the many years that have passed since that time, she has wondered how her child was getting along. She loves him dearly, but he is lost to her. He is an heir to God's potentiality, but his mother often wonders how many evils of the world he has succumbed to, and how he is meeting the issues of life. With all her heart she wishes that it were possible for her to be with her child, to fight for him, and out of her wisdom to teach him how to make the most and the best of himself. She saw him for only a few fleeting seconds, but she has a lifetime of separation in which to think about him. He is of her own flesh and blood and she loves him with all her heart, but he is lost to her forever.

May we each strive with all our might to always remain on that straight and narrow way that leads to life and happiness.

22
Excuses

As far as I know, everyone in the world wants to be a fine person. Everyone wants to be healthy, to love, to be loved, and to feel that his own life is worthwhile. However, in spite of these great longings, few of us ever come near those high goals we set for ourselves. We fail because there are so many ways for us to miss the mark.

Among the reasons for our failures are such factors as our own ignorance, idleness, indifference, indecision, negative thinking, bad attitudes, lack of enthusiasm, laziness, and irresponsibility. Probably our biggest problem is that so many of us have that very bad and very common habit of offering excuses. We are too easy on ourselves. We excuse our failures. We excuse our sins. We even excuse our excuses.

Almost everyone knows what is right and what is wrong. We have been given intelligence and a conscience to keep us from taking the wrong path. Usually we fail by the more insidious means of rationalizing, alibiing, and making excuses to ourselves in order to make whatever we are doing seem right. We excuse our lethargy, our shortcomings, our sins, and our indifference.

Another word for excuse is *alibi*. It is a kind of alias with which we disguise our failures with those names that don't identify them for what they actually are. The dictionary says that an excuse is an attempt at justification. It is a kind of apology designed to make both weakness and failure seem desirable. An excuse is a kind of substitute for performance. It is a way for us to cover up our faults without bothering our conscience. When we offer an excuse, we are making a request for an exception. We are claiming an exemption from responsibility.

When I was a young schoolboy, when a member of the class had been absent from school, he was required to bring a written excuse from a parent. Real sickness was one of the

few things that was recognized as a proper excuse. Sometimes a request might be made by the father to have his son
excused from school for a day or two to help him with the
farm work, and occasionally this request might be granted if
the student was current on his lessons and it was arranged
in advance with the teacher. Merely for a student to say
that he didn't like school or that he would rather do something else was not considered a good reason for playing
hookey.

Later on, during high school and college days, excuses
signed by parents were not required, and so the number of
students cutting classes became much greater. It has always
seemed a little strange to me that as students become more
mature and more in command of their own lives, they do
more things against their own interests. A great university
recently reported that 22 percent of its students were under
threat of being dropped because their work was less than
satisfactory. If you were to ask any of these failing students
about their problems, each one would probably have at least
a half-dozen excuses—but seldom would any of these excuses be good reason for failure.

Two adages say that "youth is not a good excuse for
one's flighty ways," and "forgetfulness is not a good excuse
for bad manners." One of our biggest handicaps is that an
excuse doesn't have to be a very good one to be accepted by
the one who makes it up. And the place where we hand in
the poorest excuses is in that most important of all schools
that we call life. But excuses can sometimes cancel out the
great virtues and destroy their wonderful opportunities.
Even intelligent people may justify in themselves such personality problems as ignorance, sloth, lethargy, dishonesty,
or indifference.

One man, in excusing his own mediocrity, said, "My
father wasn't a pusher." He felt that his friends had succeeded because of the pressure from their fathers. Others
excuse their lack of success because their parents pushed too
much, or excuse their failures by saying, "I didn't like my
boss" or "The work I was doing didn't suit me." Usually the
real reason that we don't like the boss or that the work

seems disagreeable is because we don't do our job very well. A person usually loves his job when he does it well.

Sometime ago a philanthropist went into the parks of New York City and interviewed 2,000 bums, trying to find out what causes failure. He felt that if he could find out what caused it, he could eliminate the cause. After the survey was finished, he said that each of the 2,000 derelicts told him a different story, but they all ended in the same way. They all closed their account by saying, "But I did the best I could." With their excuses, they were all disclaiming responsibility for their own failure—and that is something that we cannot do.

Recently a young man was having a little trouble getting along with himself, and he thought that he might solve his problem by the usual modern means of rebellion. He let his hair grow long and dirty, dressed himself in strange clothing, and abandoned interest in his personal appearance. Finally, he was forced to look for a job, and a prospective employer asked him to explain the reasons for his self-neglect and abandonment. The young man replied that he wanted to help those who are generally called hippies, and that he felt that if he looked like they did, he might be able to relate to them more easily.

This young man undoubtedly had a number of other reasons why he wanted to look like a hippie. He probably had some inclinations of his own to be appeased. Ordinarily, a person would not apply this logic of joining them in order to change their ways if he wanted to influence criminals, dope addicts, adulterers, or murderers.

Many people are criminals because they have formed the bad habit of trying to excuse their crimes. It has been said that there is not one guilty man in the penitentiary; those in the penitentiary usually give the excuse that they were framed or deceived. By the same process, many of us excuse ourselves for our lack of religious interest. We say, "I don't go to church because I don't want to associate with a lot of hypocrites," or "I don't go to church because my parents stuffed it down my throat when I was young," or "I don't go to church because my parents didn't encourage me to go when I was young," or "I think I can be just as good a man out fishing as I can be in church."

One of the dangers of excuses is that they are so deceptive. Like lies, they usually have some of the coloring of either truth or reason. And just as the worst lie is a half-truth, so the worst excuse is the one with enough reason in it to make it look respectable.

One of the most common of all excuses for sin is: "Everybody's doing it." And the real or imagined bad example of someone else is probably our biggest single hazard; in addition, it is one of the most common ways of condemning ourselves.

The other day I heard a minister using the scriptures to build up an official case for the excuse. He quoted those scriptures saying: "For all have sinned, and come short of the glory of God." (Romans 3:23.) "If we say that we have no sin, we deceive ourselves, and the truth is not in us." (1 John 1:8) ". . . there is none good but . . . God." (Matthew 19:17.)

Of course, these scriptures are all true, but we can greatly overdo this idea in our minds. The fact that many people are violating the laws of morality and honesty doesn't make it profitable for us or acceptable to God. Knowing the great destructiveness of evil, the Lord himself has said, "For I the Lord cannot look upon sin with the least degree of allowance." (D&C 1:31.) And again, ". . . [for] every idle word that men shall speak, they shall give account thereof in the day of judgment." (Matthew 12:36.) We increase our own involvement in sin when we take too much satisfaction from the idea that our sin is a common one. Over and over again we hear such statements as "I guess I am a sinner like everyone else" or "I'm human and I have a few weaknesses." Many people allow themselves to be sucked into more difficulties than necessary because they try to make sin seem natural, popular, and excusable. Others create another excuse for failure by adopting that popular philosophy that it doesn't matter what they do anyway. We may say that we are all a part of our environment, that our parents, our society, and our circumstances determine what we will become, and so if we don't turn out right it is not our fault.

Some say, "God knows that I wanted to do right," and they feel that this excuse will take care of everything. Or they say that God is dead or that he has lost his interest in us. Some rationalize that a just God would not hold out on them merely because they disobey a little and break a few of the commandments. Many people have said that they want to go to hell anyway, inasmuch as most of their closest friends will be there. But miseries caused by sins here make it difficult to understand how degradation can give any consolation hereafter.

The laws of God are very specific that everyone will be judged according to his works. The God of the judgment may not be very impressed with our excuses that "everybody is doing it," or that "God is dead," or that "it would not matter to him whether we went to church or not," or that "he doesn't care what kind of people we make ourselves into."

He has told us in very plain language what is right and wrong and what he wants us to do. We know that God loves good and hates evil, and certainly there is no better lead for us to follow.

23
Discord

There is an interesting passage in the scriptures in which it is said:

"These six things doth the Lord hate: yea, seven are an abomination unto him:

"A proud look, a lying tongue, and hands that shed innocent blood,

"An heart that deviseth wicked imaginations, feet that be swift in running into mischief,

"A false witness that speaketh lies, and he that soweth discord among brethren." (Proverbs 6:16-19.)

I suppose that no matter where one might go or who might be selected to put names on the seven deadly sins, one of them would always be listed as discord. In the world today we find a lot of discord—discord between nations, discord in marriages, and discord among individuals. We often allow emotional conflicts and mental strife to cause individual internal troubles. When our appetites pull in one direction and our reason pulls in an opposite direction, we feel the division and frustration of discord.

Almost all of our sins come at least partially from discord. In the scriptural statement above, the Lord mentioned first a proud look as a sin. When one is infected with conceit and has a distorted opinion of his own importance, he sows discord not only among his brethren but among everyone else. An old proverb says that "pride goeth before destruction, and an haughty spirit before a fall." (Proverbs 16:18.)

Second on the Lord's list is a lying tongue. Few things cause us more problems than lying tongues. Lying, dishonesty, and deceit have become so common that we have almost forgotten that they are sins at all. But lying is one of the most deadly of the seven deadly sins. In fact, the Lord actually mentions it twice in this particular scripture. He mentions a lying tongue as number two, and as number six he lists "a false witness that speaketh lies."

A large part of our international difficulties come because in so many ways nations try to deceive one another. Being deceitful is also one of the chief causes of both divorce and business failure. If everyone was strictly honest in meeting his responsibilities, then everyone would be far more prosperous and happier.

The Lord also hates feet that are swift in running to mischief. Many of our individual and group problems come from our self-assumed roles as troublemakers. We gossip, we quarrel, we seduce, we accuse, and we set a bad example. Someone said that the first part of his life was spoiled by his parents and the last part by his children. We often literally fulfill that awful scripture that says that a man's foes shall be those of his own household. We often act in the role of community mischief-makers and cause trouble for our neighbors and our friends. We maintain armies, police forces, and a system of courts in trying to control the troublemaking inclinations of human beings.

The Lord's list of deadly sins also mentions evil imaginations that may be centered in lust or crime or sin or sloth. No matter what they are, evil imaginations produce discords, break up families, and ruin friendships. They also cause us to lose the spirit of righteousness. They set us at odds against God and work from within to make us our own worst enemies.

Under various headings, anger and sloth (having a high content of discord) are also frequently included among the deadly sins. Jesus said:

"Ye have heard that it was said by them of old time, Thou shalt not kill. . . .

"But I say unto you, That whosoever is angry with his brother without a cause shall be in danger of the judgment. . . ." (Matthew 5:21-22.)

It might be helpful for us to try to inventory all the damage that is done, the unhappiness that is caused, and the estrangements that are brought about by angry people

117

who allow such sins as dissension, bickering, name calling, envying, jealousy, disputations, and temper tantrums to grow in their lives. These awful sins are all the offspring of anger.

In trying to justify his temper, one man said that he had to relieve his tensions by blowing his top occasionally. He thinks it helps him relieve his occupational problems by overwhelming his wife and kids with a deluge of angry, hateful, dirty words. Frequently one allows himself to become insane with anger; and after each attack of madness is past, his spirit never quite returns to where it was before. Anger breeds a whole posterity of hate, revenge, and sin.

Sloth is another of the deadly sins. Probably the highest rank that Jesus ever gave to any of the virtues was to ambition and industry, which are the opposites of sloth. Jesus came seeking the doer, the thinker, the one who was faithful to his duty. He loved those who went the second mile, those who did more than was required of them. He said that those who would inherit the celestial kingdom were those who were valiant in the testimony of Jesus. I don't know exactly what the word *valiant* means, but it might be a pretty good idea to look it up in the dictionary and see if it accurately describes our religious activity.

The most bitter denunciation that ever poured out upon the head of anyone was that which was poured upon the unprofitable servant who said, "I was afraid, and went and hid thy talent in the earth. . . ." The Master said, "Thou wicked and slothful servant. . . ." Then he said to those who were with him, "Take therefore the talent from him, and give it to him which hath ten talents. . . . And cast ye the unprofitable servant into outer darkness: there shall be weeping and gnashing of teeth." (See Matthew 25:14-30.)

The religion of the Master has to do with love, peace, beauty, righteousness, happiness, and success. He said that we should love God with all of our hearts, and that we should love our neighbors as ourselves. He has given us an unlimited opportunity to develop harmony, contentment, obedience, and fulfillment in our own lives and make them grow there as vigorously as we choose.

If we would all declare an effective war on the deadly sins and cultivate the virtues that should grow in their places, this earth would be God's paradise, and his will would be done upon the earth as it is in heaven; then all of us would be well on our way toward the celestial kingdom.

The dictionary describes *discord* as a lack of agreement, disharmony between people and things. Discord is the absence of unity. It is always identified by diversity, disagreement, contention, and unhappiness. We use the term *musical discord* to indicate that some of the participants are out of tune. Consequently there are combinations of musical sounds that strike the ear with a harsh unpleasantness. Whether one is concerned with music or with success or with a happy life, discord identifies those jarring combinations that prevent us from obtaining our goals.

Discord distracts us from doing our duty, cuts down our profits, and destroys our happiness. It can cause us to lose the spirit of worship. We can get about as much harshness from personal disagreements, quarreling, dissension, rebellion, anger, and jealousy as from the din of some savage military conflict. The reason for discord usually comes from our lack of conformity to truth and our disobedience to God.

God has said, ". . . the spirit of contention is not of me. . . ." (3 Nephi 11:29.) God is love, peace, beauty, and a happy conscience. One of the most important objectives for our lives should be to protect ourselves against the deadly sins by replacing them with the opposite virtues and abilities, including harmony, unity, concord, agreement, happiness, and peace.

24
Thy Speech Betrayeth Thee

One of the rewards of reading the holy scriptures as well as other literature is that if we understand it, every page may contain some exciting inspiration designed for our benefit. Great literature has the power to lift us upward. In his play *As You Like It,* Shakespeare points out that if we seek, we may "find tongues in trees, books in running brooks, sermons in stones, and good in everything." (Act II, scene 1.)

Jesus saw helpful sermons in the sower, the lilies of the fields, and even a prodigal son. Our world has been so designed that everything has something good to teach us.

We have another reward in literature, where, in spite of our natural blind spots, we may see the elements that make up our own human nature clearly reflected for our appraisal so that the necessary improvements may be made. Through great literature we may turn the calendar of events backward or forward so as to pick up life at its best or at its worst in any land and in any age. Therefore, suppose that we tune in on that historic long-ago night at the palace of Caiaphas, the high priest of ancient Israel, and watch and listen to what took place as though we were actually there. In this nocturnal meeting we see the scribes and elders assembled in an attempt to find enough false witnesses to enable them to rid themselves of Jesus of Nazareth. The mob has taken Jesus captive and led him to the palace of the high priest, and we see the fulfillment of the prophecy, ". . . I will smite the shepherd, and the sheep . . . shall be scattered. . . ." (Matthew 26:31.)

One of the Twelve had timidly followed along so far behind that he hoped he would not be recognized; and when he arrived at the palace of the high priest, in a further attempt to avoid being discovered, he had gone in and sat among the servants. As the accusations were being made against the Master, the spirit was taken up by the more humble members of the household, and one of the servant girls accosted Peter and said to him:

"Thou also wast with Jesus of Galilee.

"But he denied before them all, saying, I know not what thou sayest."

To get away from her he changed his location to one of partial darkness. But the record says, "And when he was gone out into the porch, another maid saw him and said unto them that were there, This fellow was also with Jesus of Nazareth."

Again he denied it, saying, "I do not know the man.

"And after a while came unto him they that stood by, and said to Peter, Surely thou art one of them; for thy speech bewrayeth thee.

"Then began he to curse and to swear, saying, I know not the man. And immediately the cock crew.

"And Peter remembered the word of Jesus, which said unto him, Before the cock crow, thou shalt deny me thrice. And he went out, and wept bitterly." (Matthew 26:69-75.)

This interesting experience of Peter points out to us that it is pretty difficult to fool people about ourselves. Probably it was not only Peter's speech that betrayed him; it was also his dress, his manner, and his general appearance. Peter had spent much of his life as a fisherman in Galilee, and his verbal expressions and his weathered look would all be quite different from those of the priests and the elders.

On one occasion Jesus said: "Who hath ears to hear, let him hear," and "By . . . seeing ye shall see." (See Matthew 13:9, 14.) But because of the blind and deaf spots that everyone has so far as he himself is concerned, we may not always understand that everyone with eyes and ears knows a lot more about us than we sometimes think. Like Peter, we imagine that we can hide a lot of things from others, whereas there may be many of our personality and character traits shouting to others to tell them *who* and *what* we are.

Frequently we even know what others are thinking, and we can predict how they will react in a given situation and whether or not we can trust them. Suppose you listen to someone talk and see how many things about him are made perfectly clear to you. Recently I listened to two boys and one girl who were trying to liberate themselves from drug addiction. They had been taken into custody a few months previously, and instead of going to the penitentiary, they had been given the alternative of putting themselves into the custody of an organization to help cure drug addiction, which invitation they had accepted.

Those being rehabilitated were permitted to live in this center as long as necessary, providing they obeyed the rules and had regular physical examinations to prove that there was no further indulgence in drugs.

As I listened to these young people tell of their experiences, and as I studied their attitudes and compared them to other young people I knew, I tried to picture what level of society they would belong with. It was easy to discover that drugs were not their only problems. Their speech, attitudes, and immaturity indicated that they also had a kind of ethical, moral, and cultural emptiness. I was sure that many of those traits that had caused them to become addicted in the first place were still present and were likely to resurface in their lives.

They told about some of the good times that they were presently having. In the center they were protected from the possible criticisms of parents and those they had wronged. They were also excused from the competition of schoolwork and occupational responsibilities. To be associated in this institution with other young people who had their same problems seemed in a way to relieve them of the blame, and their numbers seemed to give them a sense of security.

One of their present activities is to go around to various businesses, churches, clubs, and other places and solicit money to maintain themselves. They seemed to be enjoying this new adventure as though they were merely on a different kind of trip from those that they had taken while using drugs.

122

These young people were potentially capable. They had been off drugs for some time, and yet the possibility for them to ever become self-supporting, dependable citizens seemed to me, and I think it seemed to them, to be a long way off.

Again I thought about Peter trying to disclaim who he actually was because his true identity might bring with it some unpleasant disadvantage. But someday all of us are going to be judged by what we are. Then, even more than now, our speech, our appearance, our thoughts, our associates, and even our past will proclaim to everyone what and who we are.

This condition will be further emphasized when the earth upon which we live is changed to its sanctified and immortalized state. In speaking of this condition, a God-given revelation says:

"The angels do not reside on a planet like this earth:

"But they reside in the presence of God, on a globe like a sea of glass and fire, where all things for their glory are manifest, past, present, and future, and are continually before the Lord.

"The place where God resides is a great Urim and Thummim.

"This earth, in its sanctified and immortal state, will be made like unto crystal and will be a Urim and Thummim to the inhabitants who dwell thereon, whereby all things pertaining to an inferior kingdom, or all kingdoms of a lower order, will be manifest to those who dwell on it; and this earth will be Christ's.

"Then the white stone mentioned in Revelation 2:17, will become a Urim and Thummim to each individual who receives one, whereby things pertaining to a higher order of kingdoms will be made known." (D&C 130:6-10.)

In the eternal world there will be no secrets, and we will all be known for what we are. Also we will all look and act like what we are.

One of the former dope addicts said that when he was released he did not intend any further association with hippies or others who were drug-addicted. Yet he was hanging on as for his life to his sloppy manner of dress and lack of grooming. He said he had great expectations for himself in the future, and it will be wonderful for everyone if things work out that way. But the signs indicate that many of those attitudes which have caused his many problems thus far in his life are still present, and unless he makes some radical changes, he may only be betraying himself by his optimistic speech.

May God help him and may God help us to conform our lives to truth and righteousness and to God's standards of success.

25
The Underdog

Recently a complaint was being made to a state supervisory official about the activities of a certain group of individuals who were breaking the law in their business procedures. These men were making serious misrepresentations to the public, whom the state was obligated to protect. Those who were making the report were startled to hear the official say, "I am for the underdog."

The men being accused were not of the best character, but this officer seemed to feel that because their offending company was small and weak, he ought to support it. Those objecting remonstrated by saying, "We also are for the underdog, providing he is right, but just suppose that the underdog is wrong, then what?" The official said, "I am for the underdog whether he is right or wrong."

One of the reasons for the serious deterioration taking place in our society is because we condone various forms of failure. Some people have developed a sympathetic concern for weakness and encourage evil as against good. They favor the dishonest, the misfit, the pervert, the drug addict, the drifter, the ne'er-do-well, the maladjusted, the criminal, and the under-achiever as opposed to their opposites. We do great damage to both sides when we overapplaud the losers, the quitters, and the failures. We have lost our oldtime shame about either moral or financial bankruptcy. In so many ways we say, "I'm for the underdog." This attitude is expressed in a song that says, "If we fail, we fail in glory." But what kind of failure could ever be glorious?

In a very real sense every sin, every weakness, every failure, every violation of the law tends to make us underdogs or losers. And yet we encourage these traits by saying, "I am for the underdog." What we're really saying is, "I'm for the criminal against society. I'm for the rioter against the police. I'm for the minority against the majority.

I'm for the traitor against the government. I'm for the loafer against the worker. I'm for the sinner against God."

God created man to be a God-fearing, law-abiding human being, and the laws of our natures obligate us to obey God and righteousness. The Lord has tried to encourage us to make the most and best of ourselves and our circumstances at all times and under all conditions. But when we set our natures in reverse, we tend to become warped and confused, and frequently we put ourselves out of touch with the reality of our own success. There are many people whose deep-rooted sympathy with ignorance and failure make them psychotic.

Some people are greatly concerned when they hear the avowed enemies of the law scream out at an occasional report of supposed police brutality, and by this process some actually encourage the very criminals who are planning to destroy them.

We should all be against brutality in any form, and that includes that real wholesale brutality which criminals perpetrate against the people. It is becoming so serious that many people are afraid to be on the streets, and they sometimes feel unsafe even in their own homes. The most fortunate criminal is the one who is caught and punished for his first offense.

Thomas Jefferson once said, "No orderly government can be maintained without using both the principle of fear and the principle of duty. Good men obey the law because they fear the consequences." When criminals feel our weakness and disagreement among ourselves, and when they discover that the police and the public can be intimidated and pushed around, their crimes naturally become more monstrous.

Even in our churches, our schools, and our other institutions where people are trying to be helpful, we frequently hide merit by suppressing reports of excellence. We outlaw comparisons of good and poor work in school by withholding grades. We are terribly afraid that someone who doesn't do well may have his feelings hurt if his poor work is made known. Because we discredit merit, we make people ashamed and actually afraid to be superior.

Sometime ago it was reported that a young woman student was embarrassed by some recognition she had received for her scholarship. A friend said, "If you don't want to get hurt, just don't let the news be spread around." In many places we are doing a superb job in destroying excellence and promoting mediocrity. It has been said that before anyone can give much help to an alcoholic, the alcoholic must acknowledge at least to himself that he is an alcoholic and needs help. You can't help weaklings and sinners who don't know that they have a problem.

Recently a young, unmarried woman on an airplane was telling her seat companion, who was a complete stranger, that she had been living with a man for three years. To her this behavior seemed to be entirely acceptable. She said that many of her friends lived this way. The situation seemed to her to have public approval, and she proceeded to recount some of its supposed advantages. She felt no need for any religious study, for, she said, that was now out of date. She said that she was "on good terms with the man upstairs," and yet she had almost no knowledge of God or of his divine teachings. She was doing many of the very things that God had specifically forbidden and yet she seemed perfectly sure that he would approve of everything she was doing. And if he did not, I suppose it would not have mattered very much anyway.

In many other ways we are trying to make each other feel as comfortable as possible while we violate the laws of God and ignore the conventions of society to our hearts' content. Generally it isn't the wrong that we want to protect ourselves against; it is the feelings of guilt that come as a consequence.

Many have trained themselves to believe that it is smart to rebel against every kind of authority, including the God who created them and the parents who brought them into the world. And in all of these operations the criminal thinks of himself as an unfortunate underdog. He is the one who is being hunted and abused. The most serious moral breakdown in our history has been brought about because we have closed our minds to the importance of righteousness. Consequently, everyone is paying an awful price for the comfort that is being given to the evildoers. This is in great contrast to the will of God, who has said that he hates all evil and that he cannot look upon any sin with the least degree of allowance.

Another serious problem is that so many today have lost respect for good people. People don't believe in heroes anymore. Because of the sympathy people give to failure and evil, they have largely lost that ability gained in the Garden of Eden where mankind learned to distinguish between good and evil. We make our greatest contribution to wrong when we condone it.

Some 3400 years ago God came down to Mount Sinai and gave the basic law of our lives, the Ten Commandments. But a United States district judge recently ruled that a copy of the Ten Commandments could not even be displayed on a municipal courthouse grounds.

In addition to unreasonable attitudes about education and religion, many people also have strange ideas for financially penalizing the industrious and the successful in order to permit the lazy to live in idleness. Young, able-bodied men are supported on relief and with unemployment insurance while they themselves live in idleness and sin. Many believe that they have a perfect right to be just as shiftless and irresponsible as they desire while living by the efforts of others.

The time has come when we should start paying a little more attention to that part of the human family that stays on the job and does the work of producing the world's goods. And while it would not be accurate to refer to them as the "upperdogs," yet they are the opposite of the underdogs. They are the achievers, the believers, the workers, the thinkers. They are the ones who can tell the difference between right and wrong. They do their duty. They know the commandments and keep them. They have high objectives and reach them. We ought to be a little more enthusiastic about and a little more helpful to those who are responsible, to those who recognize problems and solve them. Then maybe we can help others understand that it is a lot easier to be successful when they are not wasting their time in protest marches or tearing down the establishment or overthrowing the government or shouting obscenities at the police. We also have a great deal more energy and enthusiasm for our jobs and ourselves when we are not living on relief or unemployment insurance.

The greatest idea of our world is that God created man in his own image and endowed us with his possibilities, and he wants us to be like him, to be achievers, to be doers, to be loyal, and to be fully responsible to him.

26
Rank

One of the interesting facts about our world is that its life is so highly gregarious. Men and women are at their best when they are living and working effectively and harmoniously together as races, nations, communities, and families. God's animal creations live largely in flocks, herds, swarms, and schools. Even flowers and trees grow best in groups or bunches.

In addition to living together, both human and animal life tends to establish among its members some kind of rank or order. For example, an army is divided into twenty-four different grades, beginning with the commander-in-chief at the top. Then the right of command passes down to the general of the army and continues its descent through the various grades of commissioned and noncommissioned officers and ends up with the private and the newest recruit.

The dictionary lists an interesting phrase called "the pecking order," which is described as the basic pattern of social organization within a flock of poultry. It is a natural arrangement whereby each bird is permitted to peck another bird that is lower in scale without any fear of retaliation. A separate pecking order also usually exists for each sex with all males normally dominating all females. This fact is interesting by itself; however, it becomes more important because, as the dictionary goes on to point out, a similar hierarchy of social dominance also exists among human beings.

Because of prestige, merit, authority, power, or some other kind of influence, we establish pecking orders of our own. More or less automatically a pecking order develops in families, businesses, clubs, and other organizations. Then we take advantage of these various grades of levels as we try to fit ourselves together into an intelligent, orderly pattern where everyone has a known place. For example, in a university, the governing board comes at the top and then a kind of pecking order is established that runs down through the commissioner of education, the president, the deans, the heads of departments, and so forth.

There is also a natural rating process going on among the students. In student government, athletics, and educational attainment, the seniors usually outrank the freshmen. In politics, business, the professions, and the trades, everything tends to come to its own level. We even rate our friends and associates. We begin with our best friends at the top and go down to our worst enemies at the bottom. Our various courts of law engage in a rating procedure. Persons convicted of crime pay for their wrongs by terms ranging from an entire lifetime spent in solitary confinement to only a few days with the sentence suspended.

It is interesting that most ratings are in a constant state of flux, and continual changes are always taking place. A university instructor may aspire to become a full professor; the office boy in the bank may move up to the office of president; the plowboy may become a prophet; the newsboy may become a governor. The direction of this vertical traffic is not always up. The governor may be impeached, the prophet may be beheaded, the bank president may end up in jail for embezzlement. On our various ladders of life, some people are climbing and some are slipping. It has been said that we should always be kind to those people that we pass on our way *up* to success because we may pass them again on our way down.

Of course, a person's importance may sometimes be overrated, or he may attain his standing by deceit, force, or evil. Also, one may have conflicting ranks. He may rate high as a soldier and low as a citizen. He may rank at the top of the list of businessmen and at the bottom of the list as a husband and father. And yet order and progress would not be possible in our society without some kind of a system of rating. This is also one of the ways that we have of recognizing ability and encouraging industry and integrity.

Now, just suppose that we ask ourselves a few questions about our own present and prospective rank. First, whom do we want to rate us? And second, in what areas are our greatest aspirations centered? Both of these questions may have more than one answer. The president of the United States must survive a general election in which many millions of people will express themselves. In addition, he will be rated as a husband and father by his wife and children. It is also true that each of us will be rated in many fields by several different groups of judges.

So far as I know, the finest category in which to receive a favorable rating would be to be ranked high as a great human being. It would be wonderful to be a good doctor, or a good lawyer, or a good businessman, but no rating excels that of just being a good person. It has been said that an honest person is the noblest work of God. What a thrill it would be to be a good person—one who is kind and thoughtful, one who has high aims, one who knows where he is going and how he is going to get there.

The other night I saw a television program showing some of the problems that exist among the inmates of the state penitentiary. Even among prisoners a ranking is constantly taking place. Some are becoming more hardened, brutal, sinful, and bestial. Some are indulging primarily in thoughts of revenge, hate, deceit, and evil, while others use their imprisonment as a time to clean up their lives by repentance and to prepare themselves for the future by study and proper thinking. When some prisoners are released they will carry the rank of an unreformed and dangerous ex-convict. I thought, how terrible it would be not to be capable of something better than a low ranking even among the group of depraved criminals. And just as those inside the penitentiary determine their own rank, so do we who are outside.

We are constantly grading ourselves as human beings, as employees, as husbands, as fathers, and as citizens. We are acquiring occupational rank, religious rank, and social rank. There is another interesting dimension to this rating procedure. We are not only rating ourselves for this life, but we are also determining what our rank will be for all of the eternity of time which lies before us. This makes a rating all-important.

Solomon once said, ". . . Fear God and keep his commandments: for this is the whole duty of man." (Ecclesiastes 12:13.) That makes a lot of good sense. God is our only true center of reference, our only dependable guide in the universe. If our lives can be harmonized with his in every particular, then we may predict what our personal worth, success, and happiness will be. Every good deed helps to build us up toward the primary purpose of life, for as God now is, man may become. Godliness is the highest possible rank.

For the emphasis of contrast, we might think about what it would be like to be at the bottom of the rating scale, which is occupied by hell, failure, and misery. Here Satan exists with a vast group of inferior spirits who have most seriously reduced their own rank by their practice of evil, beginning with their rebellion against God in the antemortal council of heaven. The scriptures speak to us of this lower end of the scale as outer darkness, eternal damnation, and endless misery. In God's great revelation of the final judgment, he pictured these two extremes by saying:

"He that overcometh shall inherit all things; and I will be his God, and he shall be my son.

"But the fearful, and unbelieving, and the abominable, and murderers, and whoremongers, and sorcerers, and idolaters, and all liars, shall have their part in the lake which burneth with fire and brimstone: which is the second death." (Revelation 21:7-8.)

The all-wise God of the universe has divided the eternal world into four kingdoms to harmonize with every grade of human merit and demerit. Three of these important subdivisions are degress of glory. The kingdom at the bottom, which is not one of glory, will be made up of Satan and his angels. To this large group will be added the sons of perdition, a comparatively small group made up of the worst of those who have lived upon this earth. These persons will be confined eternally in a permanent hell, and their punishment corresponds to their works of evil. Their condition has frequently been referred to as the second death.

However, by far the vast majority of earth's inhabitants will qualify for one of the three kingdoms of glory. And to make these available to as many people as possible,

God has ordained a period between the time of death and the time of resurrection when those who have seriously sinned, but not unto death, may, by repentance, suffering, and education, be purged in hell and thus qualify for the highest possible glory consistent with justice.

We should not use this important period of mortal life either to consign our eternal souls to hell or to so reduce our godliness that we may be classified among the lowest grade of the eternal beings who are saved. All of us were created in God's image. We are his children. We have been endowed with his attributes and potentialities. If we follow his directions, we have been told that we may become like our eternal parents. May we manifest the ability to overcome our sins, and thus greatly increase our rank in godliness.

27
The Process of Purification

It is very stimulating to think about that great masterpiece of invention that took place when God formed man in his own image. About the result of this creation the Psalmist said: ". . . I am fearfully and wonderfully made. . . . " (Psalm 139:14.) The most wonderful part of man is his eternal everlasting spirit, which was formed in God's image.

For a very long period prior to our mortal birth we lived with God as intelligent beings. Then at birth we were temporarily added upon with bodies of flesh and bones. The body is made of coarser materials and in some ways may be much more fragile than the spirit. In the course of living on earth for perhaps three score years and ten the body is usually worn out, and death again separates the spirit and the body. At death the body returns to the earth as it was and the spirit goes back to God, who gave it.

There is an important reason for this separation, for it gives time for the final education of the spirit and the purification of the body so that body can be made ready for a glorious resurrection. Then the body will be refined and purified and rejoined with the spirit, no more to be separated.

President Joseph Fielding Smith has said that mortality is the most important part of eternity. In this great evolutionary process called life every one of us has already passed the requirement of his first estate. Now all that stands between us and a glorious everlasting eternal life is how we handle these few years of education and testing that we refer to as mortality. Our preexistence is the childhood of our eternal lives and earth life is the time for us to grow up and pass all of the requirements that go with our mortal probation.

Edward Everett Hale once said that the best education is to be perpetually thrilled by life. We need to get a little more excited about the tremendous abilities and opportunities of our mortal existence. To begin with, we are all very important people, but we come into this life incognito. The memory of our first estate has been temporarily withdrawn so that we might have our full free agency.

As part of our wonderful mortal bodies, we have millions of blood vessels making up a circulation system, and other millions of nerves and sinews and tissues and cells with abilities and functions that only God himself could design or even understand. We have the wonderful senses of touch and smell and taste and sight and sound. Think of man's circulatory system, his communication system, his temperature control, his nervous system, the self-healing ability of his body. We have a miraculous power called procreation, by which it is possible to organize a family and beget a posterity in God's own image.

We also have a great purification system. The earth itself is a purifier. Our topsoil is loaded with all of the elements necessary to sustain life. It also has the ability to take diseases and dead plant and animal forms and change them back to their original elements. The rays of the sun kill disease and purify the earth and the air. Running water purifies itself. Vapor is taken up from the most polluted, stagnant pools and later falls again to the earth in a pure state.

The body also has many purifying devices. If we put poisons or even too much food into the stomach, it has the power to throw out the excess or those substances that are not good. Through a great system of sweat glands the body is trying to keep itself pure and healthy. The blood is also a purifier.

Someone has said that all disease is just one thing, that there aren't a hundred diseases but just one and that is an excess of waste material in the body that has not been eliminated. To illustrate, suppose you have a boil spring up on your hand. There is no point in putting liniment on the boil. If you can purify the blood underneath, the boil will go away by itself. Using this same principle, I have never heard of anyone dying of lung cancer from smoking one cigarette, but when one smokes two packages a day for a few years, his body may no longer be able to throw out the poison as fast as it is taken in. As a consequence, he has an excess of poison accumulating, which causes lung cancer. Too much cholesterol in the blood vessels may cause strokes. We are supposed to get sufficient sleep each night. Fasting also helps give the body time to purify itself.

Recently an eye doctor gave me an injection of fluorescent dye in my arm in order to find a leak in the small blood vessels in the retina of my eye. It took just a few seconds for the dye to be carried by my blood through my lungs and heart and into my eyes. Immediately after the injection was made, a great intelligence in my blood began to pick out those little foreign substances and send them through my liver and kidneys and discard them through the waste canal of the body, and within a few hours all foreign matter that the doctor had put in my blood had been completely expelled by the body's elimination process. My blood was pure again and my waste channels were clear.

I am aware that I have a good many trillion red corpuscles in my blood that are like little engineers carrying nutrition and health to every part of my system. I have billions of white corpuscles that serve as miniature medical men, constantly on guard and prepared to take immediate action should any infection or disease be introduced into my blood. In the marrow of my bones every day millions of corpuscles are being manufactured to replace those that have worn themselves out in my service.

God has given us another purifying ability in the form of repentance. Goethe once said, "I have in me the germs of every crime." We also have in us the material for every success. With repentance, we may pick out and discard the germs of evil just as the blood picks out the foreign substances and the lungs cleanse themselves of poison. Certainly repentance is an unexcelled means for maintaining our happiness. We have a great overseer of repentance in the conscience, which points the finger at impurities that ought to be expelled. The God of creation is also the God of purity. He will not permit any sin in his presence or in his heaven, and he said to his offspring, ". . . Be ye clean that bear the vessels of the Lord." (D&C 38:42.)

In 1906, the United States Congress passed the Federal Pure Food and Drug Act requiring that every ingredient that goes into our medicines must be shown on the labels. This law also makes it illegal to sell or distribute any impure foods. In like manner, God has given each of us a conscience, the power of judgment, and intelligence, and the great instructions of the scriptures designed to keep our minds, our bodies, and our spirits pure.

When the spirit cannot regurgitate those foreign elements that cause soul sickness, then all kinds of waste accumulate, which, if allowed to continue, may bring upon us spiritual disease and death. One of the greatest of our responsibilities is to learn as much as possible about what we might classify as this spiritual purifying system so that we can keep ourselves healthy at the very center of our lives. Jesus gave one of his greatest promises to those who could keep the poison out of their spiritual bloodstream when he said, "Blessed are the pure in heart: for they shall see God." (Matthew 5:8.)

The "divine pure food and drug act" might be represented in our lives by those all-inclusive words of the Savior himself when he said that we should live by every word that proceeds forth from the mouth of God. (See D&C 84:44; 98:11.) When we feed our spirits on a diet of righteousness, our bodies, our minds, and our personalities will always be strong, active, alert, and healthy. And then as a back-up law for our spiritual pure food and drug act, we have the great law of repentance by which, through an effective spiritual elimination system, our minds and hearts may throw out every foreign substance that may get into our lives.

If our stomach were to lose its regurgitation power or our physical elimination system were to wait a few months before it started disposing of its waste, it would be too late to do anything about our condition. Or when cancer cells are permitted to grow uninterrupted and to spread through the body, we soon go beyond the point of no return and the body dies. It is then returned to the purifying agency of the earth, which disintegrates the body, destroys the cancer, and returns everything to its original elements. A diseased spirit that is unable to eliminate its sins is taken to that divine purifying agency of God's hell where, by the fires of suffering, it is finally purged of the sins that it failed to get rid of by the easier and more pleasant methods of prevention and repentance.

May God bless our efforts in using these great instruments of creation to keep our minds and hearts pure.

28
Restitution

One of the greatest ideas of our world centers in the divine law of repentance. To repent is to forsake all forms of sin, ignorance, and failure, and then turn our lives upward toward more worthwhile things. By our repentance and the Lord's forgiveness we may wipe out our sins and replace all evil with good. We may dispose of the liabilities of our lives and build up the assets to our heart's desire. Isaiah gave an interesting expression to this important law when he said, ". . . though your sins be as scarlet, they shall be as white as snow; though they be red like crimson, they shall be as wool." (Isaiah 1:18.)

What a profitable situation we would find ourselves in if we had some kind of an equivalent for the law of repentance operating in our financial and political affairs. Imagine the advantage we would have if when we failed in business we could repent of the failure and wipe out the bankruptcy; or if, when we lost an athletic contest, we could repent of our lack of training, blot out the record, and start over on a new sheet with a blank score. Because repentance is such a marvelous procedure, the Lord has made it one of the first principles of the gospel.

Because of the importance of repentance, there are some things that we should understand about it, because there are ways in which repentance may lose its value and limit us, and there are other ways in which we can make it even more productive.

Repentance is similar to medicine—the earlier the disease is dealt with, the more effective the treatment will be. Even sins can be repented of in advance. An old fable tells about a horse that once ran away from his master. When the horse finally repented and returned to his master he said, "I have come back." The master said, "Yes, you have come back, but the field is unplowed." In order to make the most of the possibilities of our unplowed ground, our good deeds not done, and our accomplishments still in the dreaming stage, we must repent in advance of our lethargy, our indecision, and our sloth before they have done us any damage.

Someone has outlined some of the necessary steps of that repentance which takes place after the deed:

1. A consciousness of the wrong.
2. A genuine sorrow for the sin.
3. A determined turning away from the evil.
4. A restitution for the damage.

This last step may be one of those places where we get into the most trouble.

A story is told about a man who, during prohibition days, made over a million dollars from his rum-running operations. He violated the prohibition laws of his country and of his God with a reckless abandon, and sold liquor illegally and harmfully to a large number of people. Let's try to understand the damage that resulted as a consequence. The law of averages indicated that because of the amount of liquor he had distributed, there were probably hundreds of drunken driving accidents. Some people may have been killed under the influence of his liquor. Many people may have become immoral. Others may have become alcoholics and lost their jobs, their families, and their self-respect. Undoubtedly many other serious crimes were committed.

Although this man himself did not drink, he had reaped a very profitable harvest. After he had accumulated enough of this illicit wealth to last for the rest of his lifetime, he decided that he wanted to repent and put his own life on a respectable basis, but he didn't want to give up his evil profits. He wanted a kind of repentance with no provision in it for restitution.

This reminds us of Shakespeare's story of King Hamlet of Denmark, who was killed by his brother Claudius, who then married Hamlet's queen, ascended to the throne, and took over the kingdom. Then Claudius decided to repent

141

and obtain the Lord's forgiveness for his sins. When he tried to pray, he said:

My words fly up, my thoughts remain below:
Words without thought never to heaven go.

He said to himself, "Forgive me my foul murder? That cannot be, since I am still possessed of those effects for which I did the murder, my crown, mine own ambition and my queen." Then he asked an important question that we should know some answers to. He said, "May one be pardon'd and retain the offence?" (*Hamlet,* Act III, scene 3.)

When a thief is caught robbing a bank or stealing one's money, the first requirement that a just court would make would be to have the money returned to its rightful owner. Sometimes when one seeks the aid of the law the court asks that damages also be paid to the one who has been wronged. There is a legal phrase saying that the injured one should "be made whole." That is, he should be entitled to be as well off after he was victimized as he was before. The scriptures indicate that the Lord has some similar ideas. He certainly did not intend that his great law of repentance should be used to do wrong or work as an aid to criminals. Through Moses the Lord gave his own law of damages to make victims whole. He said, "If a man shall steal an ox, or a sheep, and kill it, or sell it; he shall restore five oxen for an ox, and four sheep for a sheep." (Exodus 22:1.)

That is, if I were to steal your sheep and you had to hire a policeman to track me down and take me through court in order to get your sheep back, you would still be quite a lot worse off than you were before. But if I were to repent of my sin and repay you by giving you four of my sheep, and agree that I would never do it again, then I might ask both you and the Lord for forgiveness of my sin. This is much fairer and a much more godly procedure.

What a wonderful world we would have if each of us made everyone "whole" that we had harmed! However, in attempting to solve one problem, we often create a few more, or jump out of the frying pan into the fire.

Recently, under the guise of repentance, a man said that he was going to divorce his wife. His reason was that he had been immoral with a third party. He said his wife was too good for him, and he didn't want to hurt her. He had decided to break up their home and let her make her own way for herself and the children as best she could. In the meantime, he intended to marry the partner of his sin, who he apparently thought wasn't too good for him. Instead of solving the problem by lifting his own standards and trying to make things up to those he had injured, he planned to do them far greater additional damage.

Suppose that this man were to completely repent of his selfishness and evil and then undertake to make everyone whole whom he had injured. If he followed the spirit of God's law, he would try to make everyone better off after his repentance than they were before. His wife would be better off if by repentance he would eliminate all the selfishness from his heart. He disliked his wife because he thought that she was better then he was, as she undoubtedly was. He was disloyal to her and treated her badly in other ways. But he could reverse all of these trends by his own reformation and by restoring his wife to the place of honor in their home that she deserves. This would not only make his family whole, but it might also make him and them holy as well.

This idea of paying back four sheep for one suggests a wonderful way for one to solve his marital problems. However, he needn't stop at four sheep. A good husband may want to put a hundred sheep up on the credit side. This would make it much easier for him to convince his wife that he is the finest man in the world, and that she should want him for her husband above everyone else in the world.

In Shakespeare's *Merchant of Venice* Portia had an even better idea. In expressing her love and devotion to Lord Bassanio, who had won her heart in love and her hand in marriage, she said:

"You see me, Lord Bassanio, where I stand, such as I am: though for myself alone I would not be ambitious in my wish, to wish myself much better; yet, for you I would be trebled twenty times myself; a thousand times more fair, then thousand times more rich; that only to stand high in your account, I might in virtues, beauties, livings, friends, exceed account." (Act III, scene 2.)

Portia was a great lady, beautiful, rich, and much sought after. But she was much more interested in *being* and in *giving* than in *getting*. There are many foolish people who think only of getting as much and giving as little as is possible. Portia was not only beautiful, high-minded, and loving, but also she knew the truth of the great law of Christ which says, "Give, and it shall be given unto you; good measure, pressed down, and shaken together, and running over, shall men give into your bosom. For with the same measure that ye mete withal it shall be measured to you again." (Luke 6:38.)

Suppose that every husband and every wife and every parent had the spirit to say to each other, "For you I would be trebled twenty times myself; a thousand times more fair, ten thousand times more rich; that only to stand high in your account, I might in virtues, beauties, livings, friends, and abilities exceed all of your fondest expectations." And suppose that we might also have that kind of an attitude regarding our relations with our eternal Heavenly Father. The Redeemer gave his life for us, and we ought to determine what we would be willing to do for him. Out of our hearts we should say to God, "For you I would be trebled twenty times myself. I would be a thousand times better as a missionary, a thousand times more honest, ten thousand times more righteous."

From the scriptures, it is clear that a two-column system of bookkeeping is contemplated in the gospel. On one side, our lives will be debited for our sins and weaknesses; on the other side we will be credited for our good works and those benefits that we bestow upon others. If we take the attitude of being as miserable and as disobedient with God as we can be, then we will become more miserable than we are. But what a lot of fun it would be to load up the credit side of the ledger and do much more than he has asked of us. Then sometime we might hear God say of us, as he has already said of a more worthy son, "This is my beloved Son, in whom I am well pleased. . . ." (Matthew 17:5.) Then it would not be long until his will would be done on earth as it is in heaven.

Section 4

"And I give you a commandment that you shall teach one another the doctrine of the kingdom.

"Teach ye diligently and my grace shall attend you, that you may be instructed more perfectly in theory, in principle, in doctrine, in the law of the gospel, in all things that pertain unto the kingdom of God, that are expedient for you to understand."
(D&C 88:77-78.)

Learning And Leading

29
The Builder

One of the most important privileges of every human being is that of selecting what he will do with his own life. He may select the occupation of his choice and decide whom he will marry and what he will make of his general situation. Outside of our dependency periods of youth and old age and the time spent in sleeping and eating, we spend more time in our occupations during our sojourn upon this earth than in any other thing.

Demosthenes said, "No one can have a high and noble character while engaged in petty and mean employment, for whatever the pursuits of men are, their characters will be similar."

Two of the most important questions that ever confront anyone are: What shall I do? And how shall I do it? It is interesting that so many of our most important activities are connected with those trades, businesses, and professions having to do with building things. We build homes, we build roads and bridges, we build pyramids, we build skyscrapers, we build sacred temples, we build character, and we build our own eternal futures.

The most important thing that anyone ever builds is people. Edwin Markham wrote:

> We are all blind until we see
> That in the human plan
> Nothing is worth the building
> That does not build the man.

> Why build these cities glorious
> If man unbuilded goes?
> In vain we build the world
> Unless the builder also grows.

The apostle Paul said: "Know ye not that ye are the temple of God, and that the Spirit of God dwelleth in you? If any man defile this temple, him shall God destroy; for the temple of God is holy, which temple ye are." (1 Corinthians 3:16-17.) No man can be engaged in a more godly business than that of building the character, excellence, and righteousness that will go with him throughout eternity.

An old legend tells of a man who interviewed some stone cutters who had different attitudes about their building efforts. To the first he said, "What are you doing?" The stone cutter said, "I am cutting stones. I work four hours in the morning and four hours in the afternoon. I am a stone cutter." To the second he said, "What are you doing?" He said, "I am cutting stones. I make four dollars in the morning and four dollars in the afternoon. I am a stone cutter." To the third he said, "What are you doing?" The third stone cutter stepped back to survey the rising walls and said, "I am building a cathedral."

Each of us is also building a cathedral, one that is far more important than a mere physical structure. As we build excellence into our work, we are also building excellence into ourselves. We are fashioning the stepping stones on which we will rise to eternal life.

A poet once said:

> A builder builded a temple
>   He wrought it with grace and skill;
> Pillars and groins and arches
>   All fashioned to work his will.
> Men said as they saw its beauty,
>   "It shall never know decay.
> Great is thy skill, O builder:
>   Thy fame shall endure for aye."
>
> A teacher builded a temple
>   With love and infinite care,
> Planning each arch with patience,
>   Laying each stone with prayer.
> None praised her unceasing efforts
>   None knew of her wondrous plan,
> For the temple the teacher builded
>   Was unseen by the eyes of man.
>
> Gone is the builder's temple,
>   Crumpled into the dust;

Low lies each stately pillar,
Food for consuming rust.
But the temple the teacher builded
Will last while the ages roll,
For that beautiful unseen temple
Is a child's immortal soul.

—Hattie Vose Hall

A number of years ago, B. H. Roberts elaborated on our eternal possibilities when he said:

"Think for a moment what progress a man makes within the narrow limits of this life. Regard him as he lies in the lap of his mother—a new-born babe! There are eyes, indeed, that may see, but cannot distinguish objects; ears that may hear, but cannot distinguish sounds; hands as perfectly fashioned as yours and mine, but helpless, withal; feet and limbs, but they are unable to bear the weight of his body, much less walk.

"There lies a man in embryo, but helpless. And yet, within the span of three score years and ten, by the marvelous working of that wondrous power within. . . what a change may be wrought! From that helpless babe may arise one like Demosthenes, or Cicero, or Pitt, or Burke, or Fox, or Webster, who shall compel listening senates to hear him, and by his master mind dominate their intelligence and their will, and compel them to think in channels that he shall mark out for them. Or from such a babe may come a Nebuchadnezzar, or an Alexander, or a Napoleon, who shall found empires or give direction to the course of history.

"From such a beginning may come a Lycurgus, a Solon, a Moses, or a Justinian, who shall give constitutions and laws to kingdoms, empires and republics, blessing happy millions unborn in their day, and direct the course of nations along paths of orderly peace and virtuous liberty. From the helpless babe may come a Michelangelo, who from some crude mass of stone from the mountain side shall work out a heaven-born vision that shall hold the attention of men for generations, and make them wonder at the God-like powers of man that has created an all but living and breathing statue.

"Or a Mozart, Beethoven, or a Handel, may come from the babe, and call out from the silence those melodies and richer harmonies that shall lift the soul out of its present narrow prison house and give it fellowship for a season with the Gods.

"Out from that pulp-babe may arise a master mind who shall seize the helm of the ship of state, and give to a nation course and direction through troublesome times, and anchor it at last in a haven of peace, prosperity and liberty; crown it with honor, too, and give it a proud standing among the nations of the earth; while he, the savior of his country, is followed by the benedictions of his countrymen.

"And all this may be done by a man in this life! Nay, it has been done, between the cradle and the grave—within the span of one short life. Then what may not be done in eternity by one of these God-men? Remove from his path the incident of death; or, better yet, contemplate him as raised from the dead; and give to him the full splendor of manhood's estate, immortality, endless existence, what may we not hope that he will accomplish? What limits can you venture to fix as marking the boundary of his development, of his progress? Are there any limits that can be conceived? Why should there be any limits thought of?

"Grant immortality to man and God for his guide, what is there in the way of intellectual, moral, and spiritual development that he may not aspire to? If within the short space of mortal life there are men who rise up out of infancy and become masters of the elements of fire and water and earth and air, so that they well-nigh rule them as Gods, what may it not be possible for them to do in a few hundreds or thousands or millions of years? What may they not do in eternity? To what heights of power and glory may they not ascend?" (B. H. Roberts, *The Mormon Doctrine of Deity,* 1903, pp. 33-35.)

Of course God is the greatest of all builders. He created us in his own image. He built this wonderful earth to serve as our home. He has organized his church upon the earth and has given those laws and ordinances that will build eternal life into all of his children. And he has invited us to

covenant with him as we build toward our ultimate goal—
eternal life.

And so, with the poet we say:

> Ah, to build! To build!
> That is the noblest of all arts;
> To build better, to build finer,
> To build more nobly—
> That gives the greatest joy, pleasure,
> And satisfaction of all arts.

May God help us to build well.

30
The American Academy of Achievement

In the United States are found many unusual and noteworthy institutions. The government itself is unique in its role among nations as a government of the people, by the people, and for the people. There is indisputable evidence that God himself raised up those wise men who wrote the U.S. Constitution and gave the nation its start toward its destiny as a free nation of free people. The early American founding fathers stand out in history as good men. They are like a forest of giant redwoods in contrast with ordinary trees. These great men, under God, established the nation upon solid, fundamental, Christian principles, and it has been given a divine mission to help keep freedom, righteousness, and human dignity alive in the world. Under the blessings of God, it has become the most wealthy nation on earth. It is also the greatest in terms of military power. It is the center of the Christian religion. More Bibles are sold each year in America than in all the rest of the world put together. Americans spend more money helping other nations than all the rest of the world put together.

Though America has a lot of problems that have not yet been solved, it is an undeniable fact that it is the world center of invention, science, culture, initiative, manufacturing, freedom, and religion, which gives its citizens corresponding responsibility.

In 1961 a unique organization was formed that carries the American spirit. This organization is called the American Academy of Achievement, which is dedicated to the development and the improvement of people. It is particularly interested in the inspiration of youth. Its purpose is to help them raise their sights, to set their goals high, and to help motivate them to excel in whatever their endeavors may be.

Each year this organization brings together approximately fifty of the most outstanding persons from

America's most celebrated occupational pursuits. These famous persons join in a meeting with several hundred of America's foremost high school honor students selected from every state in the union.

During this celebrated weekend, these accomplished present leaders are teamed up with the most promising future leaders for an intimate seminar involving an exchange of ideas and a release of the inspiration generated by the greatest accomplishment.

Theodore Roosevelt might have been anticipating the work of the American Academy of Achievement when he said, "It is not the critic who counts most. It is not the man who points out where the strong man stumbled or how the doer of deeds could have done them better. The credit belongs to the man who is actually in the arena, whose face is covered with dust and sweat and blood, who strives valiantly, who errs and comes short again and again, who knows the great enthusiasms, the great devotions, who spends himself in a worthy cause, who at best knows in the end the triumph of high achievement, and who at his worst fails while daring greatly."

At this weekend get-together, a dramatic salute to greatness is given at a dinner called the Banquet of the Golden Plate, where awards are made, praises are sung, and tributes are paid. Each year these winners include Nobel Prize laureates, Pulitzer Prize winners, recipients of the Horatio Alger Award, military heroes, artists, athletes, artisans, and actors. Some of these winners came originally from distant lands. In their own countries, some were educational dropouts, some had physical handicaps, and some lived in poverty. Even as they accept the awards, some have difficulty speaking their new adopted language. But they all have in common vision, courage, good attitudes about their country, and enthusiasm for their work. They all have ambition and industry.

There are no traitors or idlers or cowards graduating from the Academy of Achievement. No matter where they come from or what their field of endeavor may be, we commend and congratulate those who have qualified, or who will qualify, for recognition by the American Academy of Achievement.

To make the best and the most of ourselves is the purpose of life. That is also the aim of the Academy of Achievement. It is also the will of God. However, any program honoring greatness may have a shortcoming. The current greatness of businessmen, inventors, artists, actors, and athletes never lasts forever.

Alexander Pope commented on this idea of fleeting greatness when he said:

> Seeing that we are here but for a day's abode,
> We must look elsewhere for an eternal resting place
> Where eternity is the measure, felicity is the state,
>   angels are the company,
> The Lamb is the light, and God is the portion and
>   inheritance.

The scriptures point us to that eternal city where the builder and maker is God. That is why the Creator of the universe invented the idea of growth in the first place. And God has set the goal for his own Academy of Achievement to which he wants everyone to belong when he said, "Be ye therefore perfect, even as your Father which is in heaven is perfect." (Matthew 5:48.)

The American Academy recognizes those who do well in many fields of endeavor. On a much wider and more extensive scale, God not only gives awards in that much bigger business of living well, but his awards carry over beyond the boundaries of this life. He wants everyone to be learned and successful and happy.

Jesus said that we should lay up for ourselves treasures in heaven. Instead of qualifying for a Golden Plate, we can qualify for a golden life. The apostle Paul pointed out to the Corinthians that everyone will acquire a degree of glory exactly comparable to his own degree of merit. He said:

"There are also celestial bodies, and bodies terrestrial; but the glory of the celestial is one, and the glory of the terrestrial is another.

"There is one glory of the sun, and another glory of the moon, and another glory of the stars: for one star differeth from another in glory.

"So also is the resurrection of the dead. . . ." (1 Corinthians 15:40-42.)

It is interesting to try to imagine what these different degrees of glory will be like in an establishment that God himself has organized. Certainly it will in large part be based on our individual endeavor, for in the scriptures we are told that everyone will be judged according to his works. There is an important modern-day scripture that says:

"Whatever principle of intelligence we attain unto in this life, it will rise with us in the resurrection.

"And if a person gains more knowledge and intelligence in this life through his diligence and obedience than another, he will have so much the advantage in the world to come." (D&C 130:18-19.)

There are some people who are like parasites. They want to live from the accomplishment of other people. One of the first laws of accomplishment we should learn is to stand on our own feet and properly solve our own problems. Only then are we able to effectively help others.

To achieve any success, one must believe in it. Jesus made faith the first principle of the gospel; this is also the first principle of accomplishment. It is the first principle of living well. We need powerful motivations for success. We need great industry.

It is wonderful to see winners at their best. The battle cry of Babe Ruth, the great baseball player, was "It's great to be alive and to be a Yankee." Each of us should have as our personal motto, "It's great to be alive and to be a great human being." Jesus announced his mission by saying, "I am come that they might have life, and . . . have it more abundantly." (John 10:10.) That is a part of his own Academy of Achievement that we are delegated to carry out. May God help us to obtain the highest award.

157

31
Our Life's Style

Someone has said that the only unchangeable thing in the world is change. This is the common denominator in each area of life. Nothing in the world is ever static. There is an ebb and flow in the universe. Life is characterized by an upbeat and a downbeat. Society has been both the beneficiary and the victim of some great convulsive movements carrying us up and down.

While we ourselves usually set these alternating forces in motion, many of the sweeping changes that are presently taking place are adversely affecting our lives. In some places moral values are shifting. Changes are taking place in standards of education, technology, spiritual attitudes, sense of responsibility, and religious convictions. One of the most convincing evidences we might give to ourselves of any social or individual success would be to demonstrate our ability to so control these life movements that they would always serve our best interests.

President David O. McKay once said that the purpose of the gospel of Jesus Christ is to lift people upward. Its principles have been ordained by God to make bad men good and good men better. Another purpose of religion is to prevent those changes that lead people in the wrong direction. Some of our activities are presently being influenced by a powerful downward thrust. Thoughtful people are universally concerned about the negative trends that are causing so many low tides in the moral and spiritual areas of our society. Some of these downdrafts are completely antagonistic to the wisdom of the prophets. Many people are forsaking the philosophy of righteousness in a movement resembling an avalanche.

In national affairs men are parting company with some of the ideals and philosophies that sustained our founding fathers. In modern art we find work that contradicts the wholesome beauty pictured by the masters. Music has descended from the inspiring oratorios of the past to the loud, noisy mumbo-jumbo of rock music. Some modern literature fosters rebellion, violence, hate, and evil. The pedestals on which our heroes previously sat are being pulled down and their images destroyed. An attitude of degeneration from some mysterious source seems to flourish in our modern soil.

This new life-style sweeping across our world has as one of its objectives the weakening and destruction of the existing order. Some of these downdrafts are focused on promoting crime, destroying law and order, overthrowing the established order, and tearing down the government. Our finest conventions of the past are now being referred to in unsavory terms. Even the meanings of our words are being distorted.

The dictionary defines *style* as that characteristic mode that an individual uses in presenting himself. The traditional meaning of style implies an improvement in or an upswing toward beauty and quality. Style is something that gives one distinctiveness and excellence. It applies to his dress, his personal grooming, the expression of his art, and his mode of living. Style is one's manner. It is that which was formerly deemed to be most elegant or most in accord with the highest standards of social relations.

Chaucer described a high style in writing as that which was used when men wrote to kings and tried to be at their best. In addition to a high style in writing, there is also a high style in beauty, in thinking, and in living. Psychologically speaking, each individual has a life-behavior style that is typical of him personally, based on his attitudes toward others. His style may be to foster the highest social conventions—or he may have the life-style of a beggar, a criminal, or a sinner.

For many years we have trusted in an old maxim that a person is judged by the company he keeps. But we can also tell what he is by the kind of company that he sponsors within himself. We can tell many things by one's looks, his language, his attitudes, his haircut, his grooming, his manners, his actions, and his dress.

Styles are very important and can be very dangerous. There are many people who are changing God's morality styles, abandoning the style of "Thou shalt not commit adultery" (Exodus 20:14) and in its place adopting a style that says that anything goes.

Our founding fathers wrote into the Declaration of Independence a lofty sentiment, saying, "We hold these truths to be self-evident; that all men are created equal; that they are endowed by their creator with certain inalienable rights; that among these are life, liberty, and the pursuit of happiness." That is a great idea, but so many people are presently tending to reverse the direction of our founding fathers. An extended worldwide downbeat is changing the styles in government, in our living, and in our thinking. In many places people have forgotten God and done away with worship. Some say that God is dead and some say that he doesn't matter very much one way or the other.

The scriptures say that everyone will be judged according to his works. (See 1 Nephi 15:32.) Everyone will also be judged according to his example, his appearance, his influence, and his responsibility. The Lord has said that he cannot look upon sin with the least degree of allowance (see D&C 1:31), and even for every idle word that a person shall speak, he will have to give an account in the day of judgment (see Matthew 12:36). Someone may set aside the Ten Commandments, but who can set aside the consequences of sin or sloth or immorality or irresponsibility? Ignorance is a very unprofitable life-style and so is disorder.

The Lord has said, ". . . be ye clean, that bear the vessels of the Lord." (Isaiah 52:11.) Cleanliness is next to godliness, and ungodliness will always be a very serious sin, regardless of what our life-styles may be. Every human being has been created in God's own image and is responsible for his own life-style, and when we distort that image, we must be prepared to take the consequences. The sin of a corrupt life-style is not one that should be taken lightly. God is righteous, wholesome, clean, and beautiful. Satan is evil, unwholesome, unholy, and ugly.

Fundamental honesty and genuine respect for the rights of others are among the most important of the divine styles. We are all fully responsible to God, and no one has the right to do wrong. Neither does anyone have the right to do as he pleases when that harms one's fellowmen or displeases God.

God himself is our example in styling. He is the most beautiful, the most proper, the most glorious person in the universe. He has never manifested himself in any form of dirt, ugliness, or impropriety. The scriptures tell us that God is such a glorious being that no mortal in his natural state can stand in his presence and live.

"For no man has seen God at any time in the flesh, except quickened by the Spirit of God.

"Neither can any natural man abide the presence of God, neither after the carnal mind.

"Ye are not able to abide the presence of God now, neither the ministering of angels, wherefore, continue in patience until ye are perfected." (D&C 67:11-13.)

Of the occasion when Jesus was transfigured with Moses and Elias, the scriptures say:

"And after six days Jesus taketh with him Peter, and James, and John, and leadeth them up into an high mountain apart by themselves: and he was transfigured before them.

"And his raiment became shining, exceeding white as snow, so as no fuller on earth can white them." (Mark 9:2-3.)

In our own day, in speaking of his vision of the Father and the Son, the Prophet Joseph Smith said, ". . . I saw two personages, whose brightness and glory defy all description, standing above me in the air. . . ." (Joseph Smith 2:17.)

Deity serves as our example, and if we effectively follow, we may become like him and qualify for his presence in celestial glory. Obviously if we want to qualify for God's presence there will be some restrictions in our life-styles, for celestial glory is as far above the telestial as the blaze of the noonday sun is above the twinkle of a tiny star.

The Master said, "In my Father's house are many mansions. . . ." (John 14:2.) The scriptures are perfectly clear that those who inhabit the highest glories are those who have lived by the highest standards. We can be sure that when we get the right attitudes and thoughts on the inside of our lives, they will soon manifest themselves on the outside, and our excellence will eventually show itself in eternal glory.

32
Priming the Pump

The other day I ran across an interesting story that reminded me of the old days out on the farm. I would like to share it with you because it teaches a very constructive lesson that has an ennobling point of view.

There is a spot along a lonely trail in a western desert where a tin can is wired to an old pump. The pump stands there against the desert sky for anyone to see. Inside the can, a letter has been placed, written on both sides of an old sheet of wrapping paper with the stub of a pencil. The letter says:

"This pump offers your only chance for water along this trail. As of this date, June 1932, the pump is in good working order. I put a new sucker washer into it and it ought to last for another five years, . . . but when the pump is not used the washer dries out so that the pump must again be primed before it will work. I have buried enough water to prime the pump in a bottle under the white rock nearby where it will be out of the sun. So that it will not leak, I have buried it cork end up. I have made certain that there is enough water in the bottle to prime the pump providing that you don't drink any of it first.

"Instructions for priming the pump are as follows: Pour about one-fourth of the water into the pump and let it soak to wet up the leather. Then pour in the rest of the water medium fast while you pump like crazy. If you follow these instructions you will get plenty of water. This well has never yet run dry. Just have faith and follow directions and you'll be all right. However, when you get water, be sure you fill up the bottle and put everything back like you found it. Then there will also be plenty for the next one who comes along. [Signed] Desert Pete. P.S. Make sure you don't go drinkin' up the water first. If you'll prime the pump first you'll get all you can hold. However, if you drink the priming water many of the people who follow you may die of thirst."

Then this old man of the desert wrote down an interesting philosophy. He said, "And the next time you want something remember that life is like this pump. It has to be primed. I have given my last dime away a dozen times to prime my pump. Often I have fed my last beans to a stranger. It has never failed to get me an answer. You have to have your heart set to give before you can get. Pete."

It is interesting that many of the world's great prophets have lived on the desert, and our friend Pete, with his worthwhile doctrine, also seems like one whose philosophy we should make great capital out of. Jesus himself was the chief exponent of the wise philosophy that was followed by Desert Pete. Jesus said:

"Give, and it shall be given unto you; good measure, pressed down, shaken together, and running over, shall men give into your bosom. For with the same measure that ye mete withal it shall be measured to you again." (Luke 6:38.)

The farmer who doesn't put any tomato seeds in the soil in the spring doesn't get any tomatoes out of the soil in the fall. But, if he plants the seeds, the soil will do a lot better if its pump is primed with a little fertilizer and a little sunshine. It also helps if we do a little cultivating and give the tomato plants a drink of water once in a while.

In establishing America, the founding fathers put in a lot so that we might take a lot out. The national pump was primed with liberty and righteousness so that we might get out happiness and freedom. The first public building erected by the Pilgrims was not a bank or a store; it was a church where they would prime the minds and hearts of their children.

If we prime the pump with enough faith, ideals, and ambitions, then everyone will have enough and to spare. There will also be enough to leave something for those who will come after us. However, there are many people who are violating the philosophy of Desert Pete and, prompted by selfishness, they are drinking the priming water. Many don't believe in keeping the priming bottle full and building up adequate reserves. Instead of following the directions of Desert Pete, we find a new breed that wants to kill the goose that lays the golden egg. They want to pull up the pump and dynamite the well. Many have had their needs too easily satisfied without making any sizeable contribution. They have become so satiated that they don't think we will ever need any more water.

Even below the hot sands of the desert of life, God has placed some lakes and rivers of living water for our benefit. Man does not live by bread alone. And God has made available a vast supply of spiritual food and drink; but before they are accessible, we need to work the pump of faith, industry, initiative, knowledge, and attitudes.

There is something far better than a free gift of money or food or education. We are rewarded double when we develop the strength, industry, and know-how to be self-supporting. And we are sometimes better off when we have to pump our own water and dig our food out of the raw ground.

George Washington Carver lived in the days of the southern sharecroppers when it was popular to till the soil, drain from it all possible fertility, and then move on and repeat the process in some other place, always getting as much as they could and giving as little back. Some people remember George Washington Carver because he made over three hundred commercial products out of the common peanut. Others remember him because of his educational efforts among the Negroes. But I remember George Washington Carver because he said that everyone owes it to himself to leave the soil richer than when he found it.

Certainly, our hope does not lie in our natural resources, in atomic power, or in a gold supply. Our wealth is not merely rich soil, mines, missiles, and military strength. It does not lie only in full schoolhouses or satisfied hunger and quenched thirsts. The greatness of America lies in our fundamental God-motivated, well-developed human character. God does not grant us even our eternal life as a free gift. He asks us to pump a little for what we get.

There are some people who, instead of being willing to be judged by their works, want their salvation handed to them on a platter. By giving his life, Christ made an atonement for the fall of Adam. We had nothing to do with bringing about the fall and we had nothing to do with bringing about the redemption from the fall. The scripture says, "For as in Adam all die, even so in Christ shall all be made alive." (1 Corinthians 15:22.)

There is an important point here that many overlook, and that is that everyone will not receive the same kind of resurrection. Jesus himself said:

". . . for the hour is coming, in the which all that are in the graves shall hear his voice,

"And shall come forth; they that have done good, unto the resurrection of life; and they that have done evil, unto the resurrection of damnation." (John 5:28-29.)

That resurrection of damnation for those who haven't done well sounds as if it might be a great disappointment. Can you think of a more exciting idea than the resurrection of life mentioned in the scriptures? The apostle Paul writes to the Hebrews about obtaining a better resurrection (see Hebrews 11:35), and I suppose that one good way to do this would be to put more into life than we take out. In an exciting letter to the Corinthians, Paul describes the three great degrees of glory. And then he says that within these three main sections are enough other grades of glory to fit every accomplishment. (See 1 Corrinthians 15:40-42.)

In trying to make it perfectly clear that he would pay the debt of Adam's sin, the Lord said through his apostle Paul, "For by grace are ye saved through faith; and that not of yourselves: it is the gift of God: Not of works, lest any man should boast." (Ephesians 2:8-9.)

Because of this statement that our works are not necessary for the atonement, many people throw out the hundreds of passages about the value of our own works in bringing about our resurrection and leading to our eternal exaltation. Even in that next verse Paul says, "For we are his workmanship, created in Christ Jesus unto good works, which God hath before ordained that we should walk in them." (Ephesians 2:10.)

One of the best ways to get a full flow from life's abundance is to prime life's pump with faith, industry, and

166

righteousness. Only when we believe and behave and labor does life give us of its greatest abundance. When we live off someone else, we are drinking the priming water. When we tear down the establishment, we are pulling up the pump and dynamiting the well. When we rebel against God, we are causing others to choke in the desert.

There was a time when the great standards of Christianity were among the most thrilling ideas in our world. But with our acceptance of new ideas of morality and with the other evils becoming so widespread in the world, much of Christianity seems to be in the past. Most people today are only part-believers, not understanding Christian truths.

The waves of evil have washed over us until many clergymen are not actual Christians. According to several recent polls, most ministers do not believe in Christ's divinity. They do not believe in his virgin birth, his miracles, his literal bodily resurrection, or his promises of eternal life. As someone has said, many people treat him merely as some liberal "good guy." We are aware of the tragedy only as we realize that he was and is the divine Son of God who is our own eternal Heavenly Father. And nothing will prime the pump of our faith as well as living by every word that he has spoken.

How stimulating to remember the declaration of the angelic chorus proclaiming peace on earth, goodwill toward men! The angels did not have in mind the concept of the coward's peace or the traitor's peace or peace at any price.

Real peace on earth as proclaimed by the angels would not be a peace of acquiescence to evil. Christ was not a pacifist. In the antemortal existence he was the Jehovah who led the armies of God against the rebellion of Lucifer. He won the victory and cast out of heaven those who were evil. Now we must finish the job of peace and goodwill by casting all evil out of our lives. And if we expect to get a lot back, we must put a lot in. We must not be among those who say, "We will do nothing but pray and let God do everything else." May God help us to keep the pumps of our industry and faith in good working order.

33
The Vinedresser's Sons

The greatest teacher who ever lived used the parable as one of his most effective instruments of instruction. The word *parable* comes from a Greek word that means a placing beside. It is used to make ideas clear by comparing one subject that we understand with another that may be more difficult to understand. To teach us values, Jesus also used the acts of people for comparison. He compared the Pharisee praying in the streets to the publican who dared not even lift up his eyes toward heaven. He also placed the widow with her mite alongside the rich men with their abundance.

We learn many of life's most important lessons by the comparison process. Jesus used this method of teaching so extensively that Mark declares that "without a parable spake he not" unto the people. (Mark 4:34.) In the thirteenth chapter of Matthew, Jesus compared the kingdom of heaven to seven different things: to a man who sowed good seed in his field, a grain of mustard seed, leaven, a great treasure in a field, a merchantman seeking goodly pearls, a net cast into the sea, and a householder with his treasures.

In outlining the scope of the parables of Jesus, George A. Barton said:

> He spake of lilies, vines and corn,
>   The sparrow and the raven;
> And the words so natural, yet so wise,
>   Were on men's hearts engraven
>
> And yeast and bread and flax and cloth
>   And eggs and fish and candles,
> See how the most familiar world
>   He most divinely handles.

One of the primary interests of Jesus came out of his horticultural background. Horticulture has always been important in its own right, but there are many ways in which it also resembles human culture. Jesus pointed out that in both of these fields, every tree should be judged by the fruit it produces. He also said that the trees that were not productive should be cut down and cast into the fire.

He had both cultures in mind when he discussed grafting, cultivating, and other ways of increasing production. He talked about pruning out the dead, unsightly limbs and destroying the wild branches that produced poison fruit. And because the vineyard was one of the chief sources of food and drink for that day, he gave several parables in which the inspiration was centered in the vineyard.

He pictured people as the vines and himself as the husbandman who planted, pruned, and cared for them. Some vines were unproductive, and some produced wild grapes, and sometimes they themselves were spoiled. He made it clear that we should not only bear an abundance of good fruit, but that we were also commissioned to be our own husbandmen. Then he gave a provocative parable in which he used the vineyard as a means of focusing attention on such important qualities as human attitudes, daily labor, and human ambition.

The Master told of a certain man who had two sons, and to each of them he said, "Go and work in the vineyard." These boys were a part of the family and were the father's only sons. It was perfectly logical and proper that just as they shared in the benefits of the vineyard, they might also be expected to share in the duties that were necessary to produce the benefits.

People often handle their responsibilities differently. In response to the father's request, the vinedresser's first son said, "I will not go," but afterward he repented and went. In this double reaction we may read something about the character of this son. Many people are engaged in a continual round of sinning and repenting, and we are never quite sure just where they will be at any given time. The son's original refusal, even though he later changed his mind, may indicate that obedience was not one of his greatest virtues, and that he was not particularly enthusiastic about his family responsibility. We are not told why he changed his mind. There may have been some inducement offered for obedience or some penalties suggested for refusal. Sometimes in these situations family arguments are engaged in and bad feelings result while the father is trying to induce the children to carry out their part of the family responsibility. This refusal may also have been just a manifestation of the common human characteristic to avoid work as much as possible.

There are many otherwise good people who have to be bribed, coaxed, and persuaded to do their duty. It is to the first son's credit that he did change his mind and went, and he may have done it on his own power. However, his original refusal might make us wonder what he would do when the next call was made on him.

The vinedresser's second son met this situation from a completely different angle. He said to his father, "I go, sir," but he went not. Everyone who has watched human nature react to work situations is also familiar with this particular response. There are many people who characteristically promise more than they perform. In fact, their promises frequently seem to be almost completely unrelated to their performances. Many times a person making a promise can so wear out the one making the request that the work either goes undone or, in this case, the father may have to do the job for the son.

Jesus himself seemed very upset about the reaction of the second son. He compared the response to that which was then being made by the Pharisees, who have a much better record as promisers than as performers. We can well imagine the irritation of Jesus at getting only promises, inasmuch as his main mission in life was to train people to be doers of the word rather than hearers only.

In discussing this sin through which we fail to coordinate our promises and our performances, Jesus passed an interesting judgment on the Pharisees when he said, "Verily I say unto you, that the publicans and harlots go into the kingdom of God before you." (Matthew 21:31.) If the Pharisees were given a position behind the publicans and the harlots, Jesus must have intended for those who make empty promises to be placed very near the rear of the line.

I imagine that in all probability the vinedresser himself was not happy about the position taken by either of his two sons. The first son's response was a combination of disobedience softened by repentance, and the second son reacted with a falsehood and a display of irresponsibility. Fortunately these two responses do not exhaust all our possibilities for this particular situation. The answers might have been worse and they might have been better.

The parable mentions that this particular vindresser had only two sons. However, in order to explore our own possibilities and provide ourselves with a greater variety of choices, we might imagine that he had five sons instead of two. We can think of a third possibility that would be worse than either of those given. The third son might have combined the worst elements of each in his own reply and said to his father, "I won't go, " and then he could have followed up his disobedience with a continued refusal. Adding disobedience to irresponsibility represents the actual responses that many people make even to life's greatest opportunities.

A worried mother recently wrote to the writer of a newspaper trouble column. Instead of going into the vineyard to work, her son had gone into a commune for less commendable reasons. While there he acquired a wife and a baby. Then he wrote home to inquire if his parents would support the three of them until he could get a job. His mother had induced a friend of the family to offer him employment, which the friend did with the understanding that the young man would get a haircut and clean himself up a little bit. However, the boy refused the offer on the grounds that it was against his principles.

There are many people who insist that others shall do their work for them. Some purposely disqualify themselves for the battle of life and use their long hair and distorted principles as excuses for their idleness. It is like the young man who killed his parents and then asked the court for clemency on the grounds that he was an orphan. Parents or someone else will be supporting many of these kinds of people for a long time to come while they devote themselves to their distorted principles. And the number of this group that refuse their proper share of the world's work seems to be greatly increasing in our day.

But fortunately for the vinedresser, for God, and for us, there are some better choices available than any of these three. Suppose the vinedresser had said to a fourth son, "Go and work in the vineyard," and the fourth son had said, "I go, sir," and then he had gone and worked intelligently and enthusiastically until the job was done. He was not only capable, but he was also obedient and dependable. What a joy the fourth son must have been to his father, and to make a comparison, what trait could be more valuable if fully developed in us.

This sure and steady quality of always being there, of always being responsible, of always going forward is found in comparatively few people. The apostle Paul was faithful in the latter part of his life, but he fought the church in his early years. King David was called a man after God's own heart in his early life, but later he committed two of the most serious sins. Solomon was on the throne of ancient Israel when he was just a teenager. He was blessed with greater wisdom than anyone who had ever lived, and he saw God twice. Yet later in his life he disobeyed God and married some idol-worshipping women who led him away from God, and he died an idolator, very much out of God's favor. All around us we see people who possess the attitudes and lack of industry of the vinedresser's three sons. But we also see a lot of people with the characteristics of the fourth son. And even though he was not officially mentioned in the parable, we might say, "Hurrah for the fourth son!" He is the son who ought to have the gold star placed on his forehead.

But the fifth of the vinedresser's possible sons inspires us most of all. He not only said, "I go, sir," but he also went with enthusiasm and worked capably until the job was done, and he *asked* for the privilege of going. There are some people who see their opportunities as well as their responsibilities in advance and then make themselves available to perform their duties without having to be asked. The fifth son will certainly greatly please God and his father. It is probable that he will also soon own the vineyard and several vineyards surrounding it. It has been said that the world reserves its highest rewards for but one thing: initiative. This is another of those important traits of character on which the Lord has given us some timely instructions. In our day he has said:

"For behold, it is not meet that I should command in all things; for he that is compelled in all things, the same is a slothful and not a wise servant; wherefore he receiveth no reward.

"Verily I say, men should be anxiously engaged in a good cause, and do many things of their own free will and bring to pass much righteousness;

"For the power is in them, wherein they are agents unto themselves. And inasmuch as men do good they shall in nowise lose their reward.

"But he that doeth not anything until he is commanded, and receiveth a commandment with doubtful heart, and keepeth it with slothfulness, the same is damned." (D&C 58:26-29.)

As far as the actual work of the world or the work of God is concerned, most of us can do the job. Most men can learn to prune, irrigate, cultivate, and fertilize the vineyard. Most men can plant the vines and harvest the grapes. With good parents, good teachers, good companions, and good motivation, most of us can be righteous. But the most worthwhile man is the one who can do his job without having it pointed out to him. He is the one who doesn't have to be begged and coaxed and reminded to do his duty. He doesn't even need to be asked.

34
Punctuation

The lack of proper communication is one of the most common causes of divorce, business failure, educational dropouts, moral ignorance, physical disease, and spiritual weakness. As we are able to increase the effectiveness of our communication, we are able to increase the profit of our occupations, the value of our education, the quality of our character, and the excellence of our spirituality. There are many kinds of verbal, written, and mental communication that we should know more about, and we can greatly improve our general success and happiness by upgrading our ability for communication.

One of the most distinctive and meaningful parts of our communication is its punctuation. Punctuation is a system that has been invented to separate thoughts into such structural units as phrases, sentences, paragraphs, chapters, and episodes. It is also one of the best ways to clarify meaning, give emphasis to ideas, make emotions negotiable, and put expression, color, and priority into language. To assist in this purpose, people have agreed upon the use of certain marks and symbols to stand for particular meanings. Frequently we make something more understandable by underlining or by the use of accent marks or apostrophes. We often put ideas in parentheses or use quotation marks.

The story is told about a lady who bought a typewriter without adequate investigation. After only one use she promptly took it back for exchange. In her complaint she said, "Why, this typewriter doesn't have an exclamation point. I couldn't possibly use this machine, because my letters are all just full of exclamations." A typewriter without an exclamation point would have little value for this particular woman.

There are many people who use drab language and fail to get their ideas over because their communication lacks an adequate number and quality of exclamations.

An engineer was once fired from his employment. He went to the president of the company and said, "Would you please tell me why I was discharged?" The president said, "I will be very glad to. When we held our recent annual meeting you let us take the wrong course in which we lost a lot of money and so we decided to get rid of you." The engineer said, "Now wait a minute. You certainly must remember that I advised you *not* to do that." The president said, "Yes, I remember distinctly that you advised us not to do it, but you didn't pound the table when you advised us." Sometimes the quality of the conviction and the emphasis is more important than the idea itself. And just about everything depends in one way or another upon our language.

One can't even think effectively without an effective language to think with. And language can be made much more impressive, pleasant, productive, and profitable when accent marks are used to give ideas more expression and direction. Our lives themselves usually take on many of the characteristics of our speech, and we become in a sense what our communications make us.

During the nocturnal trial of Jesus, we remember the servant girl in the house of Caiaphas who said to Peter, "Surely thou also art one of them: for thy speech bewrayeth thee." (Matthew 26:73.) Our speech betrays us in a great many ways. It can exalt or depress or inspire or degrade.

One man was recently criticized because some people thought that in his thinking, in his speaking, and in his life generally, he used too many question marks where he should have used periods. This may have been the cause of one of the difficulties encountered by the Savior's apostle whom we call doubting Thomas. Thomas was one of the twelve chosen by Jesus to provide the leadership for his church. But even in such an important matter as the resurrection of Jesus from the dead, Thomas seemed to use a lot more question marks than did his associates. When the others told him that they had seen the resurrected Jesus, Thomas said, "Except I shall see in his hands the print of the nails, and put my finger into the print of the nails, and thrust my hand into his side, I will not believe." (John 20:25.) However, after Thomas had been given a personal

175

manifestation he withdrew his question marks and replaced them with some strong periods.

Today we have an almost unlimited number of doubting Thomases who continue to use question marks even after every proof has been furnished. There are so many people especially who don't believe in God or the things that God stands for, and so they just raise a lot of question marks and let it go at that. The principles of the gospel won't put much order in our lives until we have enough conviction about them to throw away the question marks and use some periods.

Someone has said, "The ability of some people to disbelieve is unbelieveable." And yet, to try to settle the great issues of life by using question marks can sometimes be pretty costly. A lady reporter for a national magazine was once asked whether or not she believed it was wrong to break the Ten Commandments. She said, "Who am I to say what is right and what is wrong?" If this young woman doesn't know whether or not the Ten Commandments are true, then what does she know? Apparently she has not eaten enough of the fruit from the tree of knowledge of good and evil. If she doesn't know whether the Ten Commandments are right and wrong, she would probably put a question mark by every other principle of truth and govern her life accordingly. When our lives are forever filled with question marks, everything else is placed in doubt. Some people have the habit of just leaving the great issues of life dangling without investigation and without making any decisions one way or the other. When we have too many question marks, the results of our lives are quite different than they are when the issues of life are fully resolved as we go along.

Many things can and should be properly and permanently settled now, and as things are settled we can put a period behind them as the appropriate punctuation for that section of our life's convictions. After Peter had said to the Master with great conviction, "Thou art the Christ, the Son of the living God" (Matthew 16:16,) he added a period. And when Jesus said to his Heavenly Father, ". . . not my will, but thine, be done" (Luke 22:42), that became the dominating philosophy of his life. The motivation for his spirit had been adopted, the issue was settled, and so he used a period. He didn't need to keep debating that point any further. When Job said to God, "Though he slay me, yet will I trust in him" (Job 13:15), he used a period, and he could proceed accordingly.

In 1852, John Ruskin wrote in his diary, "Today I promised God that I would proceed as though I believed that every principle of the gospel was true." What a great day it will be when we can get that important idea definitely and permanently settled! That might be a pretty good kind of punctuation to use even while we are gathering all the facts on which a permanent conclusion can be based. As someone has said, "If one should err in believing the gosepl of Jesus Christ to be true, he could not possibly be the loser by the mistake." But how irreparable is the loss of the person who would err in supposing the gospel of Jesus Christ to be false!

All who do evil or fail to follow gospel principles know that what they are doing is wrong, and yet they procrastinate and, for these and other inadequate reasons, they don't get these issues definitely settled with a period. Many people keep using a question mark even after they know that there is a big question mark to make the issue itself seem questionable. Next to this practice of self-deception, there is nothing quite so weakening as to have one's mind filled with question marks so that he is always in doubt when he could have great faith.

In the language of our lives we ought to use a lot of quotation marks. We can make profit greatly by using the wonderful ideas that have been developed by others. The ennobling, uplifting ideas that have been spoken and written and thought by the greatest men are available to us merely for the taking, and we can believe in them best after they have been made as much a part of ourselves as though we had thought them originally.

The scriptures give us the example of language being confounded and confused at Babel because it was corrupted. In a brighter mood, the scriptures also tell us about the time when the pure language of God will be restored for our use upon the earth. Then it will be easier to command those words that will carry the proper emotions. Before the pure Adamic language is restored we can practice so purifying our hearts and so perfecting our punctuation that our communications with our families, our friends, and God will be filled with the language of love and happiness.

35
Thinking Out Loud

One of the most productive things that we ever do in our lives is to think. Next to the immortal spirit of man, the greatest invention of all creation is that magnificent piece of machinery which is a human body. And the thing that gives both the body and the spirit its greatest significance is the brain, the mind, the ability to think.

The mind gives us that wonderful power to form ideas, to build ambitions, and to create hope in our lives. To be able to think is to be able to decide, to judge, to have opinions and convictions, and to entertain a point of view. To be able to think is to be able to love, to believe, to work, to originate, and to organize.

Plants don't think. The lives of animals are guided by the power of instinct over which they themselves have no control. Animals have a certain kind of brain that makes it impossible for a cow to learn anything except what was put there in the beginning. No generation of animals ever learns anything from any previous generation. But sometimes we tend to imitate the animals and fail to effectively use this magnificent piece of equipment with which we have been endowed.

Woodrow Wilson once commented on this weakness when he said, "The greatest ability of the American people is their ability to resist instruction." And Thomas Edison said, "There is no limit to which a man will not go to avoid thinking."

For one who has never learned how to think or who has no interest in it, thinking is one of the most difficult and unpleasant of all activities. And yet Solomon said: "As [a man] thinketh. . . , so is he. . . ." (Proverbs 23:7.) Some of the important questions that we ought to ask ourselves are: Why should we think? How should we think? What should we think about? What should we do about what we think?

The reason why we think is that that is the way we determine what we will accomplish and what we will become. Thinking, deciding, and doing are all a part of the same operation. That is how we determine our attitudes, develop our characters, build our personalities, materialize our accomplishments, and guarantee our happiness.

By this godly ability to get thoughts into our minds, we can appraise their values, make comparisons, determine their uses, make decisions, and build accomplishments. As the mind is exercised it grows strong and becomes capable of the most constructive service.

Like everything else, the mind needs exercise. It also needs supervision and direction so that it will think about the right thoughts and do the right things.

God has given us the scriptures to tell us what is right and then he has given us these potentially magnificent minds with which to put the commandments into force in order to make ourselves healthy, wealthy, wise, righteous, and happy. By the right kind of thinking and doing, we can reach any success and happiness. We can even become as God is.

Someone recently wrote to Dr. Paul Popenoe, a highly respected psychologist and writer, and asked, "In seeking a marriage counselor, what qualifications should one look for? Dr. Popenoe replied, "Start out by asking him whether or not he has made a success of his own marriage. Then get someone with the highest kind of character, a personality that you find sympathetic, and above all he must have a demonstrated ability to do the job in the right way."

Dr. Popenoe says that these abilities have little or nothing to do with how many college degrees one has or how many memberships he holds in scientific societies. One of the first requirements for an ability to think correctly and constructively is to have a well-developed sense of what is right and what is wrong. This is what we usually call character. We must also have a well-developed sense of what is profitable and what is not profitable. This we call wisdom and good judgment. Then we must have a well-developed follow-through for the materialization of our thoughts in our lives and in the lives of others. This is what we call success. Of course, to think successfully, we must have some dependable standards to go by. We have only confusion when everyone leans on his own wisdom. God is our only dependable and absolute guide in the universe. We should make sure that our judgment is always in full agreement with his.

We all need knowledge and information with which to think. Because our knowledge and information are always expressed in words, one of the basic requirements of thinking is that we have a language to think with. Some words hold more meaning than others, and some language bears bitter fruit. We need good words that take us in the right direction. We need words that are expressive and charged with power. We need words that have warmth and feeling.

Many people follow the pattern of reading great ideas aloud to themselves. By this process we can not only pass ideas through our minds, but we can also hear them as they are transformed into sound by our vocal organs. As we hear ourselves saying them, they make an impact on our ears, stir up our emotions, and become more deeply stamped into our hearts.

A great actor or speaker or musician can make his ideas, music, verse, and emotions more impressive by first hearing himself rehearse them. All great performers live their parts; they enjoy the rehearsal. And by speaking, doing, listening, and enjoying, we are also increasing our powers of memory, belief, feeling, conviction, and performance. We can learn to speak to others with greater authority, feeling, and impressiveness if we speak to ourselves as we practice. We remember a certain amount of what we think but we remember a larger amount of what we think and hear. We remember a still larger amount of what we think, hear, feel, and do.

The dictionary says that to think out loud is to utter one's thoughts without addressing anyone. Actually, when we think out loud we are addressing a very important person—ourselves. So far as our own presentation is concerned, it is likely that none of us ever has a more important audience than ourself.

Demosthenes became the greatest orator in the world by shouting his declamations to the waves, but he himself was his only listener. Coueism is a system of psychotherapy introduced by Emile Coue and based upon auto-suggestion for health and general well-being. To say and feel and believe the constantly repeated reminder that "every day in every way I am getting better and better" can bring amazing results.

Someone was once asked what he thought about a certain thing and he said, "I don't know. I haven't spoken on it yet." If we are going to speak about something, we will be more inclined to make up our minds about it. Some people speak only when they have someone else to speak to, but we ought to speak more frequently and more earnestly to ourselves, and we ought to talk more enthusiastically about more important things. We ought to memorize more uplifting ideas that have been put into the best words and sentences by others.

By this process we can stamp the best ideas into our own brain cells in such a way that they will be almost as valuable to us as though we have thought them ourselves. This is an important procedure for self-motivation, self-inspiration, and self-development.

Just as no great actor or orator would want to speak on stage impromptu and at random, so when we ourselves speak even to ourselves, we need to have some specially selected ideas and some good words to use. A great singer can most easily get the right kind of emotions into himself by singing something that is appropriate for his emotions. We can grow to love both the words and the music of those things that we know well.

Actually I get a great deal of benefit from talking to myself. I don't know that I have ever had as much good come to me from the greatest performer in the world as I have had from running my own specially selected philosophies, harmonies, and counsels through my own personality by talking to myself or thinking out loud in words I have memorized, words that have already been arranged by someone else. I can stamp my growing brain cells with the greatest philosophies, logic, prayers, and poems that have ever been developed by anyone.

Thinking out loud, using the finest words and ideas available to us, can help each of us express ourselves and our thoughts in the most appropriate language. May we always use this great tool of our loving Father in heaven.

36
Signs and Signals

The other day I took the test required to renew my driver's license. I had to demonstrate whether or not I understood what each of the highway signs means. A red octagonal sign and a red light both mean stop, and if a driver does not obey, he is liable to arrest. A yellow triangular sign means yield. Diamond caution signs warn of possible danger. White rectangular signs are for purposes of driver regulation and instruction, and a circle means that a railroad crossing is ahead.

In life, we have some non-highway signs and signals that are also designed to save our lives and increase our success. At regular intervals a Boy Scout raises his arm to the square and, with his three fingers extended, makes a sign to symbolize an oath in which he says, "On my honor I will do my best to do my duty to God and my country and to obey the Scout law; to help other people at all times; to keep myself physically strong, mentally awake, and morally straight." These words, if lived, would make our world God's paradise.

The Indians used to send important messages by smoke signals. There are many signs in nature. Geese fly south when winter is coming. The snowdrop pushes up through the snow as a sign that spring is on its way. Shakespeare said, "The weary sun gives signals of a goodly day tomorrow."

Some nineteen hundred years ago the Savior of the world looked to our day and, after telling of the many things that would immediately precede his glorious second advent, said:

"Now learn a parable of the fig tree; When his branch is yet tender, and putteth forth leaves, ye know that summer is nigh:

"So likewise ye, when ye shall see all these things, know that it is near, even at the doors." (Matthew 24:32-33.)

The red lights that signal danger are already flashing their warning, trying to induce us to put on the brakes and change our course from following that broad road leading to destruction. Million of fatalities have occurred because people have ignored signs and signals on the highway of life, and many of us are presently failing to pass our life's driving test that would guarantee safety for our eternal lives. Frequently we miss the meaning of those scriptural signals flashing from the pages of holy writ to help us make our lives more successful.

God has given us a language by means of which we can receive messages from him and also communicate ideas to and from each other. In addition to words, he has also made it possible for us to communicate with each other by means of smiles, gestures, writing, and other nonverbal signs.

We say that actions speak louder than words. Emerson once said, "I cannot hear what you say for listening to what you are."

Sometime ago I heard the story of two boys who had moved to another state to look for work. Both had previously tampered with drugs, and they had badly neglected their personal appearances. Upon arrival in their new location, they were almost immediately approached by a drug peddler and, as a consequence of their dope purchases, they were arrested and sent to jail. Later these boys were asked why they thought the drug peddler had approached them. One of them said, I suppose our appearance gave us away." Actually, these young men had plastered themselves with telltale labels telling the police and everyone else where they had been and what they had been doing, and proclaiming the kind of lives they lived. Everything that we do or think leaves its mark in our faces, on our bodies, in our mannerisms, in our movements, and even in our thoughts. Just think how easy it is to tell when someone is angry or sad or mentally ill or hurt or happy just by looking at him. Ordinarily it is very simple to tell when someone is lying or bluffing or when he is insincere or undecided.

Emerson said that beauty is the mark God has set on virtue. When one is honest, ambitious, temperate, righteous, and happy, life marks him with clear eyes and a radiant face. The Bible says, "A merry heart doeth good like a medicine" (Proverbs 17:22), but so does a virtuous character, a clear conscience, a faithful spirit, and a pure bloodstream. On the other hand, whenever one becomes drunken, lazy, immoral, and untruthful, life brands him so that he looks the part.

The scriptures speak of heavenly joy and the glory of God. There must always be a look of radiant happiness in the faces of celestial beings, and with every righteous thought that we think and every courageous deed that we do, we ourselves are growing toward God in our appearance. Conversely, whenever we do any ugly thing, think an ugly thought, or wear ugly clothing, some of the ugliness remains as a permanent part of us. It is impossible to be bad and look good. Those who have evil spirits grow to look evil. What a pity that so many people, young and old, deliberately bring about their own tragedy by making themselves ugly in their dress, their personal grooming, and their attitudes.

People with good mental attitudes, earnest enthusiasm, friendly manners, and righteous spirits are sending out to other people the finest messages about themselves. Our outside appearance must eventually become one with what we are on the inside. What we think and do is identified by corresponding manners of behavior, and our appearance always influences our behavior. By our standards of dress, our grooming, our thinking, and our doing, we qualify ourselves for the kind of company that we attract and that we are attracted to.

The other day a young man came in to talk about his narcotics problem. He had long hair and an unsightly appearance, and had taken on the appearance of his environment through the kind of people he had chosen to associate with. It was very difficult to try to get through to him the advantages of adopting a more respectable way of life. He was upset because he thought so many people were unfairly rejecting him. He said that he thought they should accept him for he was, rather than for what he looked like. I asked him to explain to me what the difference was. It never seemed to have occurred to him that one of the best ways people have for judging someone else is by looking at him and talking to him.

In trying to help him, I suggested that if he wanted to be liked for what he was, he had better make sure that he knew what kind of a person he really was and wanted to be. I suggested that he write out a detailed statement of what he now thought he was. This he could present to friends and prospective employers to correct the opinion they would develop from seeing and talking to him.

In such a paper about himself, this man would naturally have to admit that he was a dope addict. He was a dropout from education. He was lazy and irresponsible. These were facts that not even he could dispute, and these were all evident in his appearance. He was unemployed and in his present condition he would probably always remain unemployable as far as many people were concerned. I said to him, "Just suppose that we were to try to satisfy your needs and wants. You want a wife and family. You want friends. You want to feel that your life itself is productive and worthwhile. If I were to represent your prospective employer, I would certainly want to know what work you were prepared to perform, and what your character and personality qualities were. I would want to know why you had done so poorly in your school work. You might say, 'Don't judge me for what I do. Don't reject me for my poor grades, but hire me for what I am.' Those who deal with you will judge you largely by what they see, and what you are at present would probably frighten any prospective employer."

I tried to imagine myself as this young man's prospective father-in-law, but the signals I then picked up left me horrified. He couldn't support a family. He was a dropout from almost everything worthwhile, including morality. If he had lived under the law of Moses, he would have been stoned to death. Instead of loving him for what he is, it would probably be much easier to love him for what he isn't. But his most serious difficulty is that he isn't trying very hard to make any improvements.

I tried to imagine him in several other relationships, but in every case the idea was unendurable. This young man is a child of God, but he has abandoned his better self. What a tragedy when we allow that godly image in which we were created to deteriorate by neglect or the corrosion or attrition of sin. People will have difficulty accepting our logic when we say, "Don't judge me for how I look, how I think, or what I do, but judge me for what I am."

Out of India comes the idea of the aura. This is a philosophy to the effect that every individual builds around himself a particular kind of atmosphere. The quality of our atmosphere is formed by our thoughts, our attitudes, our ambitions, our personality traits, the things we love, the things that we believe in, and how we look. And certainly what one is on the outside soon gets into his insides, and what one has on his insides soon shows up on the outside. Then he transmits corresponding signals from both areas to everyone around him. When anyone comes into our presence, we are immediately conscious of a particular spirit that comes with him, and if he is wearing clean, attractive clothing, we get a better feeling about him.

When we see someone who is radiant with happiness or beaming with love or enthusiastic about his work, we get the message. We can easily recognize those who are ambitious, righteous, and full of faith. We can also clearly hear those signals of evil, failure, and ugliness. It is one of the greatest opportunities of our lives to tune ourselves in to receive the great messages that are sent out from God's presence. What a great idea it would be if we could be known by his signs and be governed by his signals.

37
Women

Women are a wonderful creation. They were designed and endowed by God for some very special purposes. In the first chapter of Genesis we read:

"So God created man in his own image, in the image of God created he him; male and female created he them.

"And God blessed them, and God said unto them, Be fruitful, and multiply, and replenish the earth, and subdue it: and have dominion over the fish of the sea, and over the fowl of the air, and over every living thing that moveth upon the earth." (Genesis 1:27-28.)

The scriptures make it perfectly clear that men and women are the spirit children of our eternal Father in heaven, and we lived for a long period with him in the spirit world before this earth was formed. Our reason makes it clear that in addition to a Father in heaven, we also have a mother in heaven. So far as we know, no one either in heaven or on earth has ever had a father without also having a mother.

The second chapter of Genesis begins by saying:

"Thus the heavens and the earth were finished, and all the host of them.

"And every plant of the field before it was in the earth, and every herb of the field before it grew: for the Lord God had not caused it to rain upon the earth, and there was not a man to till the ground.

"And the Lord God formed man out of the dust of the ground, and breathed into his nostrils the breath of life; and man became a living soul." (Genesis 2:1, 5, 7.)

Then, after ordaining the first marriage, God said: "Therefore shall a man leave his father and his mother, and shall cleave unto his wife: and they shall be one flesh." (Genesis 2:24.)

Women are very necessary to our personal success and happiness both here and hereafter. No man could be born, even in his antemortal state, without a woman. Women are ideally designed to be mothers. Generally, they are far more adept than men in caring for and training children. Women are usually more spiritual, more gentle, more loving, more moral, and more kind than men are. Traditionally, it is the men who have been the bandits, the murderers, the criminals, and the most serious breakers of the Sabbath day.

Once Napoleon was asked what the greatest need of France was. He gave the famous one-word answer: "Mothers." Another of our great needs for women is indicated when we frequently hear someone say about a young man, "The best thing that could ever happen to him would be for him to marry a right good woman." A great many books could be written on the Lord's statement that it is not good for man to be alone.

One of the areas in which men frequently run into problems is in not understanding women very well. A man once printed a book with a title *What I Know About Women*. And inside the cover, every page was a complete blank. We could get a lot more good out of women if we took the time to understand them. It would also help if we treated them better and showed them a greater amount of appreciation. Frequently our books of appreciation for women are also blanks. Women want to be appreciated, loved, and allowed to give more significant service. Men sometimes don't understand women because women are usually finer spirited than men. God himself created them to be the mothers of men, the trainers of men, the inspirers of men, the teachers of men, the companions of men, and the helpmates of men.

There is at least one woman involved in every divorce. Women often get discouraged and sad, and many of them are walking around with broken hearts. The more abuse and humiliation they have to suffer, the more mental problems and nervous breakdowns they have. In one way, women are like the soil out of which they were taken. If you want to get the most out of the soil, you must be willing to put something back into it.

It is a fundamental law that a man can't be happy unless his wife is also happy. Any performance from a man's wife will be much more satisfactory if he takes good care of her. Women are more pleasant companions and more profitable helpmates if they can operate from the top of the pedestal rather than if they are forced to crawl out from under some gloomy depression each time they offer help or give companionship.

Sometimes a woman's faith dies or her admiration dies or her trust dies or her love of her husband dies or her interest in life dies. Sometimes men not only break their hearts, but they also rob them of their virtue or kill their confidence. Then they remain only partly alive. Jesus said, "I came that [ye] might have life, and that [ye] might have it more abundantly." (John 10:10.) A part of this abundance is destroyed when a wife's respect for her husband is destroyed or when her interest in life dwindles away. The Lord said that a man and his wife should be as one. A mother and her unborn baby have a common bloodstream; and when a man is joined with a woman as one, his attributes, both good and bad, become part of her.

Tennyson once said, "I am a part of all that I have met." And because a wife is a part of her husband, her own image of herself as a woman, as a mother, and as a human being is seriously damaged when he goes wrong. There is a verse saying,

> As the husband is, the wife is.
> Thou art mated to a clown,
> And the coarseness of his nature
> Cannot help but drag thee down.

A husband's sins can make his wife physically and emotionally frigid, mentally depressed, and spiritually dead. It is very unfortunate when any woman consents to improper practices or participates in forbidden conduct, because her delicate conscience never forgets and never lets her have full peace.

One of the greatest joys that any woman ever has is to have a husband whom she can put up on a pedestal where he can be admired and loved without any inhibitions or restraints on her part. For time and for eternity every good woman likes to belong with a strong, loving, fair-minded, thoughtful, capable, righteous husband. However, she doesn't like to be unfairly dominated or have him violate her God-given rights as a person. The early American colonies never objected more vigorously to "taxation without representation" than present-day women do. Abigail Adams, wife of John Adams, once said to her husband, "Every man would be a tyrant if he could." And in this there may be a large element of truth.

Recently I talked to a husband and wife just after she had filed for divorce. He had insisted on being what he referred to as "the head of the house" but which she interpreted as unfair domination. He felt that he had to be the absolute judge about her housekeeping and her food preparation. He handled all of the money and even did the shopping. He insisted that her attendance at church deprived him of his natural rights and therefore must not be engaged in. On the other hand, the wife maintained that her husband was not capable of being the head of the house, because he was unqualified and unfair. Whenever she had an idea on any subject, he always thought that he had a better one. Whenever she expressed an opinion, he always shot it down. In many ways she acknowledged him to be a good man, but she could not endure him any longer because she felt that her rights as a person were being so badly abused.

There is great merit in the idea that one who aspires to be the head of the house, or the head of anything else, should be willing to properly qualify for the position. When one is elected to be the governor of the state or the president of the United States or the holder of any other office, it is assumed that he will keep himself qualified for the job. But even after the election, he does not get a free ride, regardless of what he does. If he begins to wreck the government or waste its assets, someone has a right to object. If he doesn't magnify his office, he may be impeached or discharged. Success in any field must be continually won.

Jesus said that only he who endures to the end shall be saved. Anyone who relaxes his effectiveness or lapses into evil may fail to be reelected, or he may be thrown out of office, or he may be compelled to endure the hateful opposition of the injured factions for the balance of his term. If one is going to take the undivided responsibility for earning a living, doing the shopping, taking care of the housekeeping, training and supervising the children, being the religious and social expert, and dictating in every other area of life, he is not only going to need an impossible amount of good training, but he will also be depriving his helpmate of some of her initiative and proper privileges.

Certainly the head of the house must know how to maintain the love of his wife, win the confidence of his children, be a good provider, and lead all members of the family to their eternal exaltation. And everyone, both men and woman, should remember that the marriage relationship must be made to work, for just as the man is not without the woman, neither is the woman without the man, in the Lord.

38
"Tora, Tora, Tora"

The other evening I witnessed a three-hour television showing of the movie *Tora, Tora, Tora,* which tells about the Japanese attack on Pearl Harbor on December 7, 1941. At that time, the United States and Japan were technically at peace. On September 30, 1938, at the Munich Conference Prime Minister Neville Chamberlain of England yielded to Nazi pressure for the division and subjugation of Czechoslovakia. Hitler also had numerous other territorial ambitions. He invaded Poland on September 1, 1939, and in that same year Japan invaded China. Hitler's army invaded Norway and Denmark in April 1940, and the Netherlands, Belgium, and Luxembourg in May 1940. Germany invaded France and France signed an armistice on June 22, 1940. And on June 22, 1941, Germany invaded Russia.

When Japan signed an alliance pact with Germany, the United States cut off Japan's foreign trade. In December 1941, Japan had a special delegation in Washington ostensibly for the purpose of bringing about more harmony between the two nations. Then on Sunday morning, December 7, 1941, without any warning and while negotiations were still in process, Japanese airplanes attacked the U.S. Naval Base at Pearl Harbor, Hawaii, where eighty-six ships were at anchor. President Franklin D. Roosevelt said that December 7, 1941, would live in infamy.

In order to get the fullest possibilities out of their crime, the Japanese attacked early Sunday morning, when many U.S. military men were off duty. As a result of this attack, some 3,500 American officers and men were killed and a great many more were wounded. In addition, great damage was done to U.S. ships, airplanes, and other facilities at the giant base. Of course, all of this was a mere drop in the bucket compared to the death and misery suffered by millions of people throughout the world because of the worldwide conflicts that took place during the following years.

Anyone who saw this moving picture would be impressed with the terrible horrors of war and the injustices committed by those madmen who bring it about. We are also impressed with what power-mad, evil dictators will do in their attempt to get control over other people.

As I watched this three-hour reenactment of these tragedies, I thought of several other things. Number one was how disastrously unprepared we are and always have been in protecting our own interests. There will always be men affected with the same kind of lust and insanity that have filled the minds of the Hitlers and the Mussolinis, the Stalins, and the Tojos. We were not prepared for the First World War and we were not prepared for the Second World War. But no matter how criminal or unfair the warlords of the aggressor nations may have been, we should have been wise enough and alert enough to have protected our citizens from the damage, horror, and death that resulted. Many of our military watchmen were not at their posts. Some of the significant known developments were not reported, and many failed to take the action they should have taken to protect the interests of the United States.

America is presently being attacked by enemies far more ruthless and destructive than any of the criminal warlords of World War II were. We are presently being bombarded by such enemies as alcohol, dope, nicotine, immorality, and atheism, which cause more misery every year than all of the wars in our history put together have ever done. These insidious enemies cause not only mortal deaths and disabilities, but also in a great many cases they destroy eternal lives as well. And we ourselves are responsible, because of our weaknesses and lack of preparation. In this regard we can think of many applications for the word of the Lord in which he said, ". . . if ye are prepared ye shall not fear." (D&C 38:30.)

While watching this moving picture, I had several other unpleasant thoughts. If we think about it a little, we soon discover that few of us are prepared for success; we are not prepared for life; and we are not prepared for death.

Some nineteen centuries ago the Son of God was sent to the earth to organize his church so that all of us could

195

belong to it and prepare ourselves for eternal life in the celestial kingdom. But the people to whom he was sent didn't do very well. Dozens of the great prophets had foretold the coming of Christ to the earth. His purpose in coming was known, and the people were warned to prepare themselves for his coming, but when he arrived, they were not ready. They did not recognize their opportunity, and even in spite of his miracles, the great doctrines that he taught, and the goodness of his life, he was persecuted and finally crucified after a short ministry of only some three years.

The antemortal Jesus also sent word to those people living on the western continent five years before he was born, telling them that he was coming and asking them to get ready to receive him. But when he arrived after his crucifixion in Jerusalem, they were not prepared. He appeared in their midst and tried to talk to them, but they were not ready. And so he dismissed them and set their meeting for a later time. He said, "I perceive that ye are weak, that ye cannot understand all my words which I am commanded of the Father to speak unto you at this time. Therefore, go ye unto your homes, and ponder the things which I have said, and ask the Father, in my name, that ye may understand" (3 Nephi 17:2-3), and then he invited them to come back the next day so that they could try again.

These people had been given a lifetime to get ready, but in spite of this, they were not prepared. And some of them spent all night long praying and planning and trying to adjust their lives in a single night for this great event which they had known about for many years.

It seems to me that this has some similarity to the attack at Pearl Harbor. If Americans had been doing their duty, they would have known about the advance of the enemy and saved this worldwide destruction. In like manner, we have been sufficiently advised about both the first and the second coming of Jesus Christ, and yet we sit stupidly unprepared and unpreparing while the enemy of all righteousness invades and decimates our ranks.

Recently I thought of this disastrous idea of unpreparedness while attending a church meeting. The clerk at the meeting was called upon by the presiding officer to come to the pulpit and speak to the people. He said, "I have been the clerk of this stake for seventeen years, and every three months when quarterly conference has been held, I have looked up at our presiding officer and thought that someday he is going to call on me to speak. That is what I thought at the first meeting seventeen years ago, but it didn't happen; and each of the sixty-seven conferences since that time I have thought, maybe it will be today. As I sat down in my chair this morning, I looked up at the president and thought it will be today that I will be called upon to address this meeting, and sure enough, this is the day that I have waited for for seventeen years." Then he hesitated and said, "But now I haven't anything to say." And everyone was aware that he was telling the truth.

However, he would have been equally unprepared at any of the other sixty-seven conferences. How much more fertile his soul would have been if he had prepared sixty-eight rousing sermons even though none of them were given to the people. But how tragically like life this is! We wallow around in our sloth and negligence until the zero hour of some great event, and then we meet stark disaster because we are not prepared.

The Lord has already sent us notice by many messengers that he is going to come again to the earth. He is going to come with his mighty angels in flaming fire to execute judgment upon all of the unrighteous. The scriptures indicate that he will come as a thief in the night, and if we are not ready to receive him, we will bring a great and everlasting condemnation upon ourselves.

The war with Japan was a bitter loss and the subsequent victory was a barren gain, because it could have been prevented from happening in the first place. But just think what we can do in getting ready for the glorious second coming of Christ. We can save ourselves suffering in this life and a condemnation that may last throughout eternity.

The Japanese moved a large military force for a very long distance without being observed, and yet there were many signs that should have put the United States on guard. A Japanese submarine was found just off Pearl

Harbor. The Japanese attack planes were observed while they were yet a long distance from Pearl Harbor, which would have given the Americans time to get fighter planes in the air and stop the attack. But the persons observing the approach just assumed that they must be U.S. planes, and they didn't take time to investigate. The Americans knew that the Japanese warlords were very unfriendly to them. They knew of their treachery in other places. They knew that they had a great concentration of ships and planes on the move. And yet the U.S. leaders allowed the Japanese to take them completely by surprise.

As I understand the title of this movie, "Tora, Tora, Tora" meant that the Japanese felt they had fully achieved their goal of taking a giant sleeping nation completely off guard. Because we are often almost entirely unaware of our most serious dangers, "Tora, Tora, Tora" would probably be an appropriate title for most of the other tragedies that wreck our lives and fortunes, for most of them could be prevented if we were on the job. We see the signs of impending destruction on every hand that are far more clear than the movements of the Japanese forces toward Pearl Harbor.

The Lord has said that he will come to execute a terrible judgment upon the unrighteous. And in our drunkenness, atheism, sloth, and irreverence, we are trying to sleep off our sins and are absenting ourselves from our posts, not even thinking about the wild-eyed, frantic concern that will be ours when we find that this tragic calamity is upon us. Then we might wring our hands and say, "Tora, Tora, Tora," indicating our complete suprise. The greatest blessings may be ours if we wake up, throw off our sins and our evil stupors, and do the works that would save our souls.

39
Trial and Error

One of the important influences in our world is a procedure known as trial and error. We try out many things with the hope that some of them will succeed. It is reported that before Thomas A. Edison succeeded in making an electric light, he conducted over five thousand experiments. During this period he was often asked, "Have you found it yet?" And he would reply, "No, but I have found a lot more ways that won't work." Mr. Edison learned something from each experiment, and he finally succeeded in lighting our world.

Trial and error has accounted for a great deal of progress in the field of medical science. In medical laboratories, dogs, rats, mice, and guinea pigs are used for experimentations. To everyone except the animals themselves, this technique of trial and error seems like a fine idea.

We have another procedure that is closely related, in which we use ourselves as guinea pigs. However, this process does not work out very well. Trial and error with a ratio of five thousand failures to one success was a very profitable operation in discovering the electric light, and to destroy five thousand guinea pigs in order to save one human being might also be thought of as being worthwhile. But this kind of a ratio would not be a very effective way to discover an effective form of government or to build a happy marriage or to learn how to live successfully.

Recently a man who is sixty-four years of age came seeking help after he had just been fired from his job. He was sorry about how many of his trials had turned out to be errors, and he kept repeating the phrase, "I wish I could live my life over again." But how ridiculous can one get, for no one can live his life over again.

There are no rehearsals in life. There is no good way to try out crime. We can't rehearse birth, or life, or death. We must not only be right the first time, but we must be right all the time, or we must suffer serious and unpleasant consequences.

There are many things that can be learned by a process of trial and error. On the other hand, that is the worst way to learn some things. Someone has said that anyone who learns only from his own experience is a fool. It is much more profitable to learn from the experiences of others.

To live successfully, trial and error is usually not only unprofitable, but it is also unnecessary. That is, when it was discovered that strychnine would kill, it became forever unprofitable for anyone else to perform that guinea-pig function for himself. Because God understands the importance of this idea, he has given us some alternatives that are much safer and far more beneficial. He has marked out a straight and narrow way that will lead us unerringly to life eternal. He has told us everything that is good for us to do, and he has given us detailed descriptions of those things that should always be left undone.

If one desires to live successfully, there are certain things that he just must not do. The best illustration of this important success principle took place when God was attempting to make the greatest nation in the world out of the descendants of Abraham. He released them from their Egyptian bondage and then assembled them at the foot of Mount Sinai for instructions as to how they should proceed.

Then the Lord came down to Mount Sinai in a cloud of fire, and the mount quaked and the people trembled. He gave to Moses, their leader, the following commandments:

1. Thou shalt have no other gods before me.

2. Thou shalt not make unto thee any graven image.

3. Thou shalt not take the name of the Lord thy God in vain.

4. Remember the Sabbath day to keep it holy.

5. Honor thy father and thy mother.

6. Thou shalt not kill.

7. Thou shalt not commit adultery.

8. Thou shalt not steal.

9. Thou shalt not bear false witness.

10. Thou shalt not covet.

If these ten commandmants were strictly obeyed, almost any nation could be the greatest nation. But when they are disobeyed, no nation has a chance. For even God cannot make a great nation out of liars, thieves, killers, adulterers, Sabbath day violators, and those who dishonor their parents and disobey God.

How ridiculous it is to waste our lives experimenting with those things for which we already have the answers! When Cain made himself a guinea pig and tried out murder, he found it to be extremely unprofitable, with terrible consequences for himself. Lucifer proved that rebellion was not a good way to solve problems, and as a consequence of his error he lost forever the very things that he sought most.

It was by a process of trial and error that Judas Iscariot discovered how bitter and unprofitable disloyalty is. Disobedience to God is always our greatest error. The prophet Samuel said that "to obey is better than sacrifice" (1 Samuel 15:22), and obedience is always better than using ourselves as guinea pigs to solve problems that have already been solved. It has been proven over and over again that no one can live successfully by trial and error.

After a person has married and had five children, it is pretty late to decide that he has married the wrong person. I recently talked with a couple who during the first ten years of their marriage had been very happy, but the second ten years have been a nightmare of misery. A happy beginning does not necessarily guarantee a happy ending. On the other hand, some marriages have started poorly but later they have turned out gloriously.

Learning by trial and error usually involves large numbers of trials, and frequently the errors become established as habits before the experimentation is finished. Many people have destroyed themselves in a few months while trying out harmful drugs. Even in this greatest of all ages of wonders and education, the walls of penitentiaries, reform schools, and hospitals are bulging with people who have tried out crime, dope, sin, and weakness for themselves.

There are many people who through trial-and-error procedures have become enmeshed in the modern epidemic of rebellion. And many have thrown overboard valuable social conventions that have been successfully tested for ages. Many people consistently ignore the tested and proven principles and strike out on a voyage of discovery for themselves despite the fact that past experience has shown they will find only disappointment.

In the past we have prided ourselves on law and order, decency and beauty, education and religion, but now even these are under attack by some misguided, inexperienced persons bent on some form of trial-and-error experimentation, with the government, other people's property, and other people's welfare as the guinea pigs.

We all want to change our circumstances, but few of us want to change ourselves. However, our attitudes must be changed before we are enslaved by our errors. As a part of trial and error, many people make the mistake of putting government and religion and God on trial. Actually, God cannot be put on trial. Religion is not on trial; marriage is not on trial; sex is not on trial. We are the ones who are on trial, and only to the extent that we live by the correct principles that have already been discovered will we be able to determine our own success.

Henry Ward Beecher once said that religion had not been tried and found wanting—it had been found hard and not tried. If we would like to experiment with a system of success that has no errors in it, we might try out the pure religion of Christ. The finest success program ever known was not discovered: it was revealed—and it has been given its implementation by the Master himself. With all of the right answers available, he has said, "Follow me," and every human being will finally be judged by how well he carries out that single direction.

*"... he who doeth the works of
righteousness shall receive his reward,
even peace in this world, and eternal
life in the world to come."
(D&C 59:23.)*

Our Goal:
Eternal Life

40
The Spirit of Success

The most marvelous invention of God himself is a great human being. It was by his authority and permission, based on our own antemortal excellence and our promises of faithfulness for this life, that each of us was individually authorized to have the tremendous experiences of this mortal probation. Our mortality is the middle estate in that godly plan for the evolution of our lives, and the end objective is that we should aspire to become even as God is.

Henry Van Dyke has pointed out that no one is ever born into this world whose work is not born with him. Each of us who has been given a share in the benefits of this life has also been allotted a part of the responsibility for carrying on the necessary work of the world. God's approval for us to have this privilege is also based on our obligation to carry out our part of the work of the Lord. Each person has an inherent responsibility to himself and to God to make the most and the best of his own life.

One of the best ways to reach success in life is to get into our hearts as soon as possible the spirit of success. This word *spirit* is a very interesting word. Probably its most important meaning is to describe the essential part of a person. The Bible says that God is a spirit, and those who worship him must worship in spirit. The most important part of anyone is his person, which is an immortal spirit. This is the intelligent, animating, deciding part of us.

During our mortality as well as after our resurrection, we are spirits *and* bodies. And while no one ever sees his own spirit during his mortality, yet we know that that is the most important part of us. The Bible says: "But there is a spirit in man: and the inspiration of the Almighty giveth them understanding." (Job 32:8.) Of death it was said, "Then shall the dust return to the earth as it was: and the spirit shall return unto God who gave it." (Ecclesiastes

12:7.) At the resurrection, the spirit and the body will be inseparably connected, no more to be separated.

The dictionary gives another meaning of spirit. We refer to spirit as our motivation, the mood we set, the attitude we adopt. Our spirit is closely related to our disposition. One may manifest low spirits in terms of discouragement, depression, or despair, or he may manifest high spirits in terms of vigor, courage, firmness, or mettle. Spirit means ardor, enthusiasm, and animation. It is the essence of that energetic activity of the inner person. The spirit is what activates the body. It is also the most active ingredient in any success.

One of the important personalities in the government of the ancient Babylonian empire was Daniel, the Israelite captive. The reason for his preferment is given in the record, which says: ". . . Daniel was preferred above the presidents and princes, because there was an excellent spirit in him; and the king thought to set him over the whole realm." (Daniel 6:3.)

In making this statement, Darius, the king of Babylon, was probably anticipating Shakespeare, who said, "I care not for the limbs, the thews, the stature and the bulk and the big assemblances of a man." He said, "Give me the spirit." When this spirit of success gets into a lot of people, we call it "esprit de corps." That is the spirit of the corps. It is a sense of union, common interest, and common responsibility. It is found among people with spirit.

There is a religious spirit. The Bible says that the fruits of the spirit are love, joy, peace, truth, and righteousness. One of the greatest gifts of God is the ability to build up our own spirits to their highest levels. Spirit builds up our success, and success builds up our spirits. A consciousness of our own skills gives us great enthusiasm and whets our appetites for still greater accomplishments.

While the conspirators were plotting the death of Julius Caesar, Cassius was telling them of some of Caesar's weaknesses, in the light of which he could not understand how Caesar had risen to such great heights. He told of one occasion when Caesar had challenged him to swim the

Tiber, but when they were only a part of the way across the river, Caesar gave out and cried, "Help me, Cassius, or I sink." Cassius turned around in midstream and rescued the emperor, then swam to shore with Caesar on his back. On another occasion while the army was in Spain, a fit of epilepsy came upon Caesar. Cassius told how Caesar's eyes lost their luster, his lips lost their color, and the great tongue that bade the Romans write down his speeches in their books became as that of a sick person. Cassius knew of these weaknesses and was disturbed about why Caesar had so far out-distanced him in greatness. Cassius said:

> . . . this man
> Is now become a god, and Cassius is
> A wretched creature, and must bend his body
> If Caesar carelessly but nod on him. . . .
>
> Why, man, he doth bestride the narrow world
> Like a Colossus, and we petty men
> Walk under his huge legs and peep about
> To find ourselves dishonorable graves.

And then he said:

> Now, in the names of all the gods at once,
> Upon what meat doth this our Caesar feed,
> That he is grown so great.
> —*Julius Caesar,* Act I, scene 2

That is a good question, because greatness does feed upon certain things. For one thing, Caesar fed on courage. He said:

> Cowards die many times before their deaths;
> The valiant never taste of death but once.
> Of all the wonders that I yet have heard,
> It seems to me most strange that men should fear;
> Seeing that death, a necessary end,
> Will come when it will come.
> —*Julius Caesar,* Act II, scene 2

All great men adopt particular diets to vitalize their spirits. By reading great literature and memorizing important ideas, we may feed on the best qualities of other men. We may also get the Spirit of the Lord himself by feeding on his word, carrying out his ideas, and keeping his commandments. Faith and righteousness may stir our minds

207

with more powerful ambitions and put more power into our souls. Success, greatness, enthusiasm, and righteousness are vitalizing foods that strengthen our souls.

When speaking about his sleepy disciples in the Garden of Gethsemane, Jesus said, ". . . the spirit indeed is willing, but the flesh is weak." (Matthew 26:41.) However, the flesh can become fully subservient and willingly obedient to a strong spirit, and the spirit of the success of one may reach out to help others.

After the death of the courageous Julius Caesar, the spirit of his great leadership went on to defeat the conspirators. Finally Brutus, the chief conspirator himself, decided to give up the fight. As he was about to commit suicide out of fear, he said:

> O Julius Caesar! thou art mighty yet!
> Thy spirit walks abroad, and turns our own swords
> Into our own proper entrails.
> —*Julius Caesar,* Act V, scene 3

Brutus did not surrender to the enemy army nor to its leaders, Anthony or Octavius, but to the ghost of the courageous Caesar. Brutus said:

> The ghost of Caesar hath appear'd to me
> Two several times by night; at Sardis once,
> And this last night, here in Philippi Fields.
> I know my hour is come.
> —*Julius Caesar,* Act V, scene 5

And that is how many men feel when they lose their spirit and become seriously discouraged. When we begin to lose the spirit, we usually begin also to lose our righteousness, our faith, and our eternal salvation. Many of our most serious tragedies come when, like Brutus, we become spiritless. Then we are as though we have lost our appetite for good things. Then we no more hunger for success. Our bodies become too unwieldy for that which animates them.

The story is told of three medical students trying to make a cadaver stand up against the wall of their medical laboratory so they could more effectively study him. Each time, just as they thought they had him properly balanced on his own two feet, he would slump down to the floor again.

After several tries, one of the students said, "I know what is the matter with this dummy—he hasn't any spirit in him." That may be about what God thinks of us when he tries to get us up on our feet to stand up for righteousness and truth and, by our own actions, to make something worthwhile of ourselves. When we have in our hearts and personalities too much weakness and ignorance and too many sins, we tend to keep slumping down onto the floor because of lack of spirit.

Sometimes our spirits get sick and their strength is decimated by one of the dread spiritual diseases, such as doubt, discouragement, sin, weakness, despair. Sometimes we hear of people who have had their spirits broken or their faith destroyed, and as we get negative attitudes or rebellious hearts or disobedient wills, the spirit is overpowered and loses its ability for righteousness and accomplishment.

One of the most unpleasant of all experiences is to see someone lose his spirit. A little discouragement or a little self-pity or a little sin can often break down morale. Then it is easy for one to lose interest in himself or in his employment or in his family—or even in God. I know of a fine young man who grew up amid the greatest kind of opportunities, but he became infected by the wrong attitudes. After a few successes he began to take some unrighteous privileges. His employer tried to talk to him about the detrimental effects of what he was doing, but he took offense at these corrections and felt that the employer had shown poor judgment. Little by little the young man developed a sour spirit that made him worse than useless to his firm.

When we do the wrong things, we lose the spirit of doing the right things. Then we get the spirit of failure and death. The greatest blessing in the universe is to live—to live better, to live more nobly, to live more righteously, and to live profitably.

We can enlarge our own abundance by increasing the strength of our spirit and of our success. We can read the holy scriptures and other great books. We can memorize the finest philosophies of success. We can listen to the most inspiring music and do the greatest deeds. "There is nothing that succeeds like success. Nothing is so inspiring as success.

Nothing is so hygienic as success. Nothing so advances the welfare of human lives as success."

May we stamp our minds with the spirit of love, the spirit of righteousness, the spirit of service, and the spirit of happiness.

41
Your Estate

In the monthly letter of the Royal Bank of Canada, one subject for discussion was entitled "Building Your Estate." After reading this interesting discussion, I looked up the various meanings of the word *estate*. In one definition the dictionary says that estate refers to the state of condition of things. It is a form of existence or a state of being. Another meaning of the phrase "your estate" is one's material possessions.

Some people either waste or spend all that they earn so they never know the thrill of developing an accumulation. Some have a philosophy similar to that of the government, in which they actually spend more than they earn. Actually, everyone should build up several different kinds of estates. Of course, one must have a material estate, even if it consists only of the clothes he is wearing. But people feel much more secure if they also have something put away for a rainy day.

When we fail to accumulate sufficient for our needs, we feel insecure and live under a cloud of fear. God made it possible for everyone to be wealthy. With a working span of forty years and an annual income of $8,000, a man may earn $320,000 during a working lifetime. If he works harder and more effectively, the amount may be much greater. We sometimes speak of someone as being worth his weight in gold. If you weigh 150 pounds, your value in gold at $35.00 per troy ounce would be $76,000. If, as you grow older, you put on another fifty pounds, you could increase your value to $102,000. So over your lifetime you may earn at least three times your weight in gold. Of course, taxes will take some of your earnings, some will be wasted, and much of it will go to provide for your family and personal needs. Some of it may also be saved to build up a personal estate.

It was a very wise man who once said, "A part of all you earn is yours to keep." In our time we don't talk as much as we used to or as much as we should do about the advantages of thrift, and yet a little thrift can turn our lives upward in so many ways. James J. Hill, the great railroad builder, once said, "If you want to determine whether you are destined to be a success or not, you can easily find out. The test is simple and infallible. Are you able to save money? If not, drop out. You will fail as sure as fate, for the seeds of success are not in you." In order to have enough to save, we must work a little harder and plan a little better.

Closely related to estate building is the concept of compound interest. This is a financial device that can be made to work for us effectively night and day, and one of the finest satisfactions is to put away some of the fruits of our toil and then see compound interest continue to work for us at an accelerating speed and be available for whatever assignment we may choose to give it, including making our lives comfortable in our later years.

The poet said, "Grow old along with me! / The best is yet to be, / The last of life, for which the first was made." (Robert Browning, "Rabbi Ben Ezra.") Usually there is a period at both ends of life when we are dependent upon someone else. This can be more than offset during that long period in the middle of life when we can earn more than we consume.

There are two primary ways to produce an income. One is by our own labor, and the other is by employing our money to work for us. In spite of its advantages we sometimes belittle money and call it by such unpleasant names as filthy lucre or tainted money. We talk about money as the root of all evil. However, the lack of it is at the root of many of our marital and family problems. Like men, money as such is not evil. It can be made to promote either good or bad.

Before we can properly judge whether money is good or bad, we need to know how it was obtained and what it is to be used for. If it is used to provide homes and educations for our children, or if it is used to give us peace and comfort in old age, we would certainly say that it is very good. Someone once tried to demean its powers by saying that "money can't buy happiness." His friend replied, "Maybe not, but it does enable one to pick out the particular kind of misery that he enjoys the most." Someone else has commented that if one can't buy happiness with money, it must be because he just doesn't know how or where to shop.

It is true that some wealthy people have been hurt by the unwise use of money, and an even greater number of poor people have also been hurt by the unwise use of money. However, there are also untold millions of people who have been severely hurt by poverty. When properly used, money is a good thing, no matter whether one is rich or poor.

We should always keep in mind the limitations of money. Money is preserved labor. It is stored-up accomplishment. It is industry made negotiable. It may even be the liquidation value of ourselves.

The minute we started our life's work we began using up our life's energy, and when it is gone, our mortal lives are over. As we carry on our life's work, we are exchanging the energy of life for money. Money is not only the best medium of exchange for other things; it is also a medium of exchange for us.

Recently a factory bought an expensive machine that had a contemplated life expectancy of ten years. The management established a depreciation fund and each year put ten percent of the machine's value aside so that the machine could be replaced when it was worn out. Our estate is our depreciation fund, and the part that we put away may represent the best part of ourselves, since what we save comes from the top of our income. That is what is earned in the highest strata of our ability.

I know of a young woman who inherited a small estate from her parents. All her life she had loved them dearly. They had been devoted to her. From their labor they had provided her with food, clothing, and shelter. They had had her teeth fixed, bought her eye glasses, and paid the expenses of sending her to school. When they died, they left to her the unused portion of their lifetime of toil. To her this was something sacred, and she could not think of wasting it or spending it frivolously. It had been wisely invested, and the income came to her each month from her parents, who

213

were continuing to help her just as they had during her lifetime. By means of this living trust, they had achieved a kind of economic immortality, and the benefits from their lifetime of labor would go on forever.

As a medium of exchange, money can be used as an effective bartering agent and can be exchanged for all good things. This stored-up labor can help to get children through college and send them on missions. It can build temples. It can help to provide old people with medical care and many comfortable experiences during their declining years.

The fund that we build up as we wear out can go on helping others even after our own lives have been exhausted. This not only represents a great opportunity for us; it also presents us with an important moral and religious obligation. The apostle Paul said to Timothy, "But if any provide not for his own, and specially for those of his own house, he hath denied the faith, and is worse than an infidel." (1 Timothy 5:8.) By building up an estate, we can provide for our families even after we are gone.

The apostle James said, "Pure religion and undefiled before God and the Father is this, To visit the fatherless and widows in their affliction, and to keep himself unspotted from the world." (James 1:27.) James had in mind that when we visit the needy, we should have something of value in our hands, for he said, "What doth it profit . . . if one of you say unto them, Depart in peace, be ye warmed and filled; notwithstanding ye give them not those things which are needful to the body. . . ?" (James 2:14, 16.)

There are other kinds of estates besides financial. We have an estate of time. At birth men and women are granted an average time estate of three score years and ten, which may be used as they desire. Time is the raw material out of which all other successes are made, and one reason why the life insurance industry has become one of the world's largest businesses is because it can supply the needs of our beneficiaries if our time should be cut short. Men don't buy life insurance only because they will die. Primarily they buy life insurance because some of their loved ones will live.

There is another kind of estate, which we might call our spiritual estate. Among our most important properties are our godly traits of personality and character. Jesus was talking about an eternal state when he said that we should lay up for ourselves treasures in heaven. He pointed out a fortunate group of people who were rich toward God. One of the arguments against earthly treasures is that we can't take them with us, and one of our greatest good fortunes is that we can build a spiritual estate that we *can* take with us. In a direct revelation, the Lord himself has said, "If a person gains more knowledge and intelligence in this life through his diligence and obedience than another, he will have so much the advantage in the world to come." (D&C 130:19.) We can take character with us. We can also take righteousness. We can take love and memories and happiness. We can take our families. The family relationship was ordained to be eternal, and if we want to be great souls in heaven, we should practice being great souls on earth.

In building our eternal estate, we might try to estimate what a wonderful eternal companion and a family of faithful, loyal, dependable, loving children would be worth. It might be interesting to try to place an estimate on how much eternal happiness is worth or what one's eternal value might be as a parent or a marriage partner or a citizen or a loyal child of God.

These are just a few of those treasures mentioned by Jesus that qualify us for eternal life in the presence of God. He has said that eternal life is the greatest of all of the gifts of God. He has said that he that has eternal life is rich, and so he is. The greatest joys, the finest satisfactions, the most perfect love that we can develop or be worthy of may be taken with us. What a thrill that each one of us can become rich toward God and enjoy that heavenly estate in those mansions that he has already prepared for us!

42

Incarnation

One of the great wonders of life is our language. Before anyone can think very well, he needs a language to think with. Language is made up of words and sentences and ideas. If we are masters of our thought, we may endow our words with greater color and more meaning and then we may put them together in such a way as to instill more worthwhile convictions, inspire higher dreams, and build more noble characters.

We have a productive word that is not often used, called *incarnation*. The dictionary says that to incarnate is to embody, to invest with a bodily nature or form. Its most prominent meaning and most frequent use refer to the fact that the antemortal Jesus, though he was the Son of God, had a spiritual body, and ruled with his Father in the councils of heaven, was incarnated in flesh, and began his mortality in a manger in Bethlehem. One scriptural passage announcing this fact says:

"In the beginning was the Word, and the Word was with God, and the Word was God.

"The same was in the beginning with God.

"All things were made by him; and without him was not anything made that was made.

"In him was life; and the life was the light of men.

"And the light shineth in darkness; and the darkness comprehended it not. . . .

"And the Word was made flesh, and dwelt among us, (and we beheld his glory, the glory as of the only begotten of the Father,) full of grace and truth." (John 1:1-5, 14.)

In other words, his immortal spirit was clothed with a mortal body of flesh and bones.

Certainly nothing is more clearly written in the scriptures than the fact that the life of Christ did not begin at Bethlehem; neither did it end on Calvary.

He said, "I came forth from the Father, and am come into the world; again, I leave the world, and go to the Father." (John 16:28.)

On the night before his death on the cross, he prayed in the garden to his Father, and in his prayer he said, "I have glorified thee on the earth: I have finished the work which thou gavest me to do. And now, O Father, glorify thou me with thine own self with the glory which I had with thee before the world was." (John 17:4-5.)

It is just as certain that our lives do not begin when we are born, and they will not end when we die.

The Bible tells us of two creations. The first was a spiritual creation or birth that took place in heaven. This creation is recorded in the first chapter of Genesis, where we are told that the spirit of man was formed in the image of God. Then in the second chapter of Genesis is found the account of God's forming the body of man out of the dust of the ground to serve as an earthly tabernacle for his spirit. For the period of our mortality this is a temporary connection. At the time of death the spirit and body are separated for a time in order to better prepare both the body and the spirit for resurrection, when they will be joined together, no more to be separated. One of the great privileges of life is that we have this tremendous association of an eternal spirit incarnated in an earthly tabernacle of flesh and bones for the benefit of both.

On the other hand, we remember the account of that great antemortal war in heaven when Lucifer, the brilliant son of the morning, allowed rebellion to get into his heart so that he drew away one-third of all of the hosts of heaven after him, and they were cast out of heaven and were denied the opportunity of a physical incarnation. They could never be added upon with a mortal body and so they would never have a resurrection. (See Jude 6; Revelation 12:7-9; D&C 29:36-37; Abraham 3:27-28.) Consequently, these evil spirits try to get possession of the bodies of other people. We remember that out of the body of Mary Magdalene Jesus cast seven devils. (See Luke 8:2.)

There are other meanings for the word *incarnation.* Someone has said that Martin Luther incarnated the spirit of the reformation into the people of the world. We use this same idea in other ways. We try to incarnate the spirit of the gospel as an actual force in our lives. We try to get into ourselves the spirit of righteousness, the spirit of accomplishment, the spirit of kindness, and the spirit of happiness.

We may also incarnate into ourselves the most stimulating ideas and elevating ideals. Some people have incarnated in their own souls the spirit of beauty and the spirit of happiness. Actually, each one of us may incarnate within himself many influences of good and bad. Edwin Sanford Martin put this idea in verse under the title of "My Name is Legion." He said:

> Within my earthly temple there's a crowd;
> There's one of us that's humble, one that's proud,
> There's one that's broken hearted for his sins,
> There's one that unrepentant sits and grins,
> There's one that loves his neighbor as himself
> And one that cares naught for fame and pelf.
> From such corroding cares I would be free
> If I could once determine which is me.

When we incarnate influences of both good and bad, confusion and failure result. We should thus strive to incarnate within ourselves only those character qualities and personality traits most beneficial to our own interests. Greatness consists largely in how successful we are in this incarnation enterprise. We might think of our attitudes, skills, and habits as a great company of invisible angels working in our interests day and night and making up the facets of our multiple personality. We may incarnate those powerful angels of enthusiasm, angels of faith, angels of ambition, and angels of industry.

There are many tender and holy emotions that also, like ministering spirits, are available to be embodied by those uplifting acts we ourselves may initiate. There are many rich and lovely flowers of thought that may be made to spring up in us, bearing productive eternal seed. The great virtues, loyalties, and righteousness cannot live by themselves. To have power, they must be incarnated in some person.

Conversely, life has some punishments for those evil influences in us. When one becomes an alcoholic, his punishment is that a ruinous driving thirst pushes him further and further down the road to despair. That is, the alcoholism incarnates itself, and wherever the person goes, forevermore the awful burden of his sin will go with him. If one tells lies, his sentence is that he will become a liar. If a man thinks negative thoughts, the evil of his negativism takes control, and he soon discovers that he has a negative mind that he cannot cleanse himself of. One who thinks depraved thoughts develops a depraved mind. One of the important lessons that we should try to learn in life is that once evil has gotten into us, it is pretty difficult to get it out. Jesus commanded the seven devils to come out of Mary Magdalene and they obeyed. But that is not so easy with the evil attitudes and habits that we allow to get possession of us.

John the Revelator talks about that time when this awful situation will become complete and permanent. He said, "He which is filthy let him be filthy still. . . ." (Revelation 22:11.) To live with filth is bad enough, but to have filth live in us is much more horrible.

One of the greatest opportunities of our lives is to have ourselves possessed by happiness, beauty, righteousness, and godliness. May God help us with these important incarnation procedures, that we may incorporate the greatest qualities into our eternal souls.

43
Easter

Once each year we observe that very important day we call Easter. On this historic occasion we commemorate one of the most significant events in all of human history, which took place over nineteen centuries ago in a garden tomb on the outskirts of Jerusalem. It was on that day that Jesus Christ was resurrected from the dead, and, as Matthew reported in the scriptures, "the graves were opened; and many bodies of the saints which slept arose, And came out of the graves after his resurrection, and went into the holy city, and appeared unto many." (Matthew 27:52-53.)

This is more than ordinarily important to us, because it has been divinely appointed that everyone who ever lives upon this earth must sometime die, and God has given us the assurance that everyone will also be resurrected. The scripture says, ". . . it is appointed unto men once to die, but after this judgment." (Hebrews 9:27.) And Paul declared, "For as in Adam all die, even so in Christ shall all be made alive." (1 Corinthians 15:22.)

The greatest of all human concepts has to do with this idea of the immortality of the personality and the eternal glory of the human soul. We have an interesting custom among us that when some friend or loved one dies, we assemble together in a memorial service to express our love for the departed and recount some aspects of the great doctrines embodied in the Easter message.

Someone has said that there are three primary purposes that might be served at the funeral of a loved one. First, it gives us the privilege of expressing love and respect for those who have departed this life. It has been said that there are no ordinary people, and if we could see the mortality veils drawn aside of the most ordinary person, we might better understand his great natural worth. It might also help us to a greater appreciation of ourselves. The apostle Paul once said that we should be careful how we entertain strangers because some have entertained angels unawares. (See Hebrews 13:2.) But it wasn't very many years ago that all of us were in the presence of God, and to be his children makes all of us very important people.

The second purpose to be served at a funeral service is to offer all possible comfort to the bereaved. This is a little bit more difficult. God makes no duplicates. Every individual is unique and serves a unique purpose in the world. It is proper that we should grieve at the death of a loved one and more especially for those who lack the hope of a glorious resurrection.

The third purpose of a memorial service is that it gives us an opportunity for meaningful meditation and contemplation about the purpose of our own lives and how we might motivate ourselves to make better preparation for that great experience when it will happen to us.

It has been pointed out that the three most important dates in anyone's life are the following:

First, the day that he is born. The early American philosopher Henry Thoreau once said that we should thank God every day of our lives for the privilege of having been born, and then he went on to speculate on the supposition of what it might have been like if we had not been born. Just suppose that you had never been born. Try to enumerate all of the wonderful joys and great experiences that you would have missed as a consequence. However, what Mr. Thoreau may not have known was that one-third of all of the children of God never were born because they failed to pass the requirements of their first estate. And yet for some very good reasons every spirit child of God hungers for a body. The unembodied spirits who appeared to Jesus in his day preferred the bodies of swine rather than to have no bodies at all.

The second most important date in life is the date we are married. That is when a new family comes into existence. God ordained marriage for time and for all eternity, and he established the family as our important human institution.

And the third most important date is the date of one's death. Death is the gateway to immortality. It is our graduation day into eternal life. We frequently miss one of our greatest benefits because we don't like to think about death. To most people, death means unpleasantness, and we don't like to think about unpleasant things. However, if we think enough about death in advance, and review those dozens of scriptural passages about the literal bodily resurrection, we will make more adequate preparation for it.

Harry Emerson Fosdick once said, "If the death of the body forever ends all there is to human life and personality, then the universe would be throwing away with utter heedlessness its most precious possession. A reasonable person doesn't build a violin with infinite care, gathering the materials and shaping the body of it so that it can play the composition of the masters, and then by some whim of chance-caprice smash it to bits. Neither does God create this great masterpiece of human life and then when it has just begun to live throw it utterly away."

President John Quincy Adams was a great believer in immortality of the soul. A short time before his death he was met by a friend on the streets of Boston, and the friend said to him, "Mr. Adams, how are you?" The former president replied, "John Quincy Adams himself is quite well, thank you, sir, quite well indeed. But the house in which he is living is becoming quite dilapidated and is tottering on its foundations. Time and the seasons have almost destroyed it. The roof is warped and worn out, the walls are so shattered that they tremble in every wind. The old tenement is becoming almost uninhabitable and I think I shall have to move out of it quite soon. But John Quincy Adams himself is quite well, thank you, sir, quite well indeed."

When Victor Hugo was eighty-three years of age he said, "You say the soul is nothing but the resultant of my bodily powers. Why then is my soul more luminous when my body powers begin to fail? Winter is on my head but eternal spring is in my heart. I breathe at this hour the fragrance of the lilacs, the violets, and the roses as at twenty years. The nearer I approach the end, the plainer I hear around me the immortal symphonies of the worlds which

222

invite me. It is marvelous yet simple, it is a fairy tale yet it is history. For half a century I have been writing my thoughts in prose, verse, history, satire, ode, and song. I have tried all, but I feel I have not said a thousandth part of what is in me. When I go down into my grave I can say like many others, 'I have finished my day's work,' but I cannot say I have finished my life. My day's work will begin on the next morning. Death is not a blind alley. It is a thoroughfare. It closes up the twilight, it opens upon the dawn."

At another time he said, "Let us not forget and let us teach it to all that there would be no dignity, that it would not be worthwhile to live if annihilation were to be our lot. What is it that alleviates, that renders men strong, wise, just, at once humble and aspiring, but the perpetual vision of a better world whose light shines through the darkness of the present life? As for myself, I believe profoundly in a better world and after much struggle, many hardships, and numerous trials, this is the supreme conviction of my reason as it is the supreme consolation of my soul."

The Son of God came to earth in the meridian of time and established his church with the idea that everyone should belong to it, and if we believe and live those great doctrines of faith, repentance, baptism, the gift of the Holy Ghost, and his other laws of righteousness, we may qualify ourselves for the celestial kingdom of God. The celestial kingdom is that eternal kingdom that Paul refers to in his famous first letter to the Corinthians as the glory of the sun. It surpasses in glory the other two kingdoms of glory, as the glory of the sun is above the light of the moon or the twinkle of a tiny star. The celestial kingdom is the order to which God himself belongs, and if we live the principles of the gospel, we may entitle ourselves to the better resurrection mentioned by Paul.

We know quite a bit about celestial people. A number of them have appeared upon this earth, and each time those who have received them have said that they are impossible to describe, that their brightness and glory defy all description. The angel who came to announce the resurrection of Jesus was described as being like lightning and dressed in raiment white as snow. When the resurrected Jesus came forth from the tomb and confronted the Roman soldiers who had been placed there by Pilate to maintain the security of the tomb, they became as dead men. This was not because they were timid, easily frightened men. There were hard, bold, courageous, seasoned soldiers of Rome who had been taught to stand in the presence of death without ever a quiver of emotion. But now, when they stood in the presence of a resurrected, glorified being, they became as dead men.

Some sixty years after this event, the resurrected Jesus appeared to John the Revelator on the Isle of Patmos. The revelation says that John was in the spirit on the Lord's day when he heard a voice behind him as the voice of a trumpet. He turned to see who had spoken to him, and he said that he saw "one like unto the Son of man, clothed with a garment down to the foot, and girt about . . . with a golden girdle. His head and his hairs were white like wool, as white as snow; and his eyes were as a flame of fire; And his feet like unto fine brass, as if they burned in a furnace; and his voice as the sound of many waters." (Revelation 1:13-15.)

The great program of salvation teaches us that if we are faithful, we may become even as God is, and may our lives guarantee that it may be so.

44
The True and Living Church

The most important event that ever took place upon this earth was when the Son of God was sent here to be the Savior of the world and the Redeemer of men. He organized his church upon the earth with the instruction that everyone should belong to it. As he was preparing to ascend unto his Father in heaven, he said to the chosen apostles, "Go ye therefore, and teach all nations, baptizing them in the name of the Father, and of the Son, and of the Holy Ghost: . . . and, lo, I am with you alway, even unto the end of the world." (Matthew 28:19-20.)

Those who were authorized to carry on in his name were given the priesthood, which is the authority delegated to man to act in the name of the Lord. In our own day, the Lord has referred to his church as the only true and living church upon the face of the earth.

During his ministry in Jerusalem, the Lord taught the people by the use of parables. We might think of the comparison involved in his statement concerning the true and living church. People in the electrical industry speak of a "live wire," which is a wire that is connected with the source of power. When a business organization is prosperous, successful, and meeting the purposes for which it was organized, we say that it is alive. When it ceases to render service and can't pay its bill, it dies. It is also true that civilizations perish and even churches can lose their authority and become dead forms as far as the divine source of power is concerned.

There have been many occasions in the long, unhappy period of this earth when God has withdrawn his power and authority from men. In the days of his personal ministry upon the earth, he gave us a clear understanding of the characteristic features of his church, some of which are as follows:

1. His church should be called by his name, and the things that are done in it should be done in his name. If it does not bear his name, it is not his church. He said, "And how be it my church save it be called in my name? For if a church be called in Moses' name then it be Moses' church; or if it be called in the name of a man then it be the church of a man; but if it be called in my name then it is my church, if it so be that they are built upon my gospel." (3 Nephi 27:8.)

2. His church was built upon the foundation of apostles and prophets, Jesus Christ himself being the chief cornerstone. Any church that does not have this foundation cannot be his church.

3. He specified men to carry part of his divine authority. The scripture says, "And he gave some, apostles; and some, prophets; and some, evangelists; and some, pastors and teachers; For the perfecting of the saints, for the work of the ministry, for the edifying of the body of Christ: Till we all come to a unity of the faith. . . ." (Ephesians 4:11-13.)

4. Those who minister in his name must be divinely called and must bear the authority of the priesthood. They must not call themselves as though they were choosing some occupational or recreational pursuit. Paul said, "And no man taketh this honour unto himself, but he that is called of God, as was Aaron." (Hebrews 5:4.) Jesus himself said, "Ye have not chosen me, but I have chosen you, and ordained you. . . ." (John 15:16.)

5. No one ministering in church affairs has any right to teach his own doctrine. Jesus himself said, ". . . I seek not mine own will, but the will of the Father which hath sent me." (John 5:30.) Every authorized servant of the Lord should teach only those doctrines authorized by Jesus Christ. He put great emphasis on adhering strictly to truth and not teaching fables or the doctrines of men. He seriously condemned those who teach confusing, unauthorized, and contradictory doctrines that lead so many astray. It is not merely a matter of someone being a good man or not. He must have authority from the Lord.

6. One of the indispensable features of the true and living church is continuing divine revelation. It must be established on the principle of continual revelation from God. After Peter with great enthusiasm had declared to Jesus, "Thou art the Christ, the Son of the living God," the Savior said to him, "Blessed art thou, Simon Barjona, for flesh and blood hath not revealed it unto thee, but my Father which is in heaven. And I say also unto thee, That thou art Peter, and upon this rock I will build my church; and the gates of hell shall not prevail against it." (Matthew 16:16-18.) Upon which rock? Certainly it was not the rock of Peter. The Lord did not build his church upon the rock of any man. He built his church upon the rock of *revelation*. When the power of revelation is cut off, the church degenerates into a purely human institution. What an awesome picture is presented when man-made church organizations are all proclaiming that there will never be any more revelation, that the canon of scripture is full, that the record of those three years of Christ's ministry are all we need for our guidance, in this greatest of all dispensations.

The holy scriptures tell of many revelations that will be given by God in the future. It tells of many heavenly visions that must come to the earth. For example, through Malachi the Lord said, "Behold, I will send you Elijah the prophet before the coming of the great and dreadful day of the Lord: And he shall turn the heart of the fathers to the children, and the heart of the children to their fathers, lest I come and smite the earth with a curse." (Malachi 4:5-6.)

On April 3, 1836, at the dedication of the temple in Kirtland, Ohio, the Prophet Joseph Smith recorded the fulfillment of this prophecy of Malachi when he said:

"After this vision had closed, another great and glorious vision burst upon us; for Elijah the prophet, who was taken to heaven without tasting death, stood before us, and said:

"Behold, the time has fully come, which was spoken of by the mouth of Malachi—testifying that he [Elijah] should be sent, before the great and dreadful day of the Lord come—

227

"To turn the hearts of the fathers to the children, and the children to the fathers, lest the whole earth be smitten with a curse—

"Therefore, the keys of this dispensation are committed into your hands; and by this ye may know that the great and dreadful day of the Lord is near, even at the doors." (D&C 110:13-16.)

7. One of the identifying marks of the true church is that the Lord sends out his missionaries two by two without pay. Even though they work for nothing, they are not authorized to teach their own ideas.

8. The Lord ordained marriage to be our primary institution. When the first marriage was performed, death had not yet entered the world. The authority to marry was included in Peter's commission when the Lord said, ". . . whatsoever thou shalt bind on earth shall be bound in heaven. . . ." (Matthew 16:19.) However, since the apostasy from God and the long black night of the dark ages, ministers have acted without this authority and have inserted a bill of divorcement into the sacred marriage covenant when, as they conclude this sacred ordinance, they say, "Until death do you part." Only to the true and living church has the Lord revealed the sacred ordinances that must be performed in a temple dedicated to the work of the Lord.

9. The church of Jesus Christ taught the great doctrine of salvation for the dead. Millions of good people have died without a chance of hearing the gospel in this life, and the Lord has provided a program for teaching them in eternity. They may also have the necessary ordinances performed by an authorized servant in holy temples built for that purpose. If any church does not teach this important doctrine, it is not the true and living church. This doctrine was taught by Jesus and also by Peter, who said, "For for this cause was the gospel preached also to them that are dead, that they might be judged according to men in the flesh, but live according to God in the spirit." (1 Peter 4:6.) It was taught by the apostle Paul, who said, "Else what shall they do which are baptized for the dead, if the dead rise not at all? why are they then baptized for the dead?" (1 Corinthians 15:29.) These and other passages of scripture indicate that baptism

228

and other ordinances were being administered vicariously for those who did not have the opportunity to perform these sacred ordinances for themselves.

A minister of an unauthorized church was recently conducting a funeral for an infant child who had died before reaching the age of accountability. The minister said to the parents and to the congregation that this child would be forever lost, that he would be condemned by the Lord, and that his parents would never see him again. This is not a part of the gospel of Jesus Christ; it is a manmade doctrine, for Jesus called little children to him and said, ". . . of such is the kingdom of God." (Mark 10:14.) This condemnation, fostered by Satan, is not only a wicked and false doctrine— it is also a very cruel doctrine.

God is just and fair, and when his children have been deprived of their opportunities in this life, they will have a chance to be instructed and learn the necessary lessons in the spirit world. His great eternal world is a place of happiness and glory, but it is also a place of learning and understanding.

It is helpful for anyone engaged in identifying the true and living church to make a list of those distinctive doctrines taught by the Master, a few examples of which are given above. The true and living church will be the one that embodies and practices all of these principles. People make a very serious mistake when they tell themselves that they believe the New Testament to be the word of the Lord and then, one by one, reject some of its most important doctrines. It is easy to accept the Bible when it is closed and sitting on the shelf; it is much more difficult when it is opened and people are face to face with the great doctrines that they have ignored or denied. Either we should accept all of the doctrines taught by the true and living church or the New Testament should be abandoned. The Lord has given no doctrines that are untrue, unimportant, or superfluous, and when we make up the doctrinal blueprint for the true and living church, there must be no doctrines missing and there must be none left over.

45
The Lord's Prayer

Different things have different meanings to different people. Certain ideas may have great significance in the lives of some individuals, but to others, these same ideas may be like pearls cast before swine. A few words may alter the entire viewpoint of one person, whereas another may read something from beginning to end without any noticeable change taking place in him. Socrates pointed out that before a philosopher speaks, he should always have his words steeped in meaning, and we who are eager to gain the good things of life should always have our minds filled with understanding.

One of the most significant idea combinations is found in the Lord's Prayer (Matthew 6:9-13), the greatest sermon ever given. This prayer is sixty-four words long and can be read in a quarter of a minute. However, Jesus frequently "wrote between the lines," and his meaning often went out into the "margins." Many of his words and ideas are symbols that stand for something else. The sacrament of the Lord's supper stands for something more important than itself. Baptism is also a great symbol fraught with the deepest meaning and significance. The cross is also important for what it makes us think about.

Many of us have recited the Lord's Prayer by heart since we were children, yet its meaning has frequently gone over our heads, leaving us unchanged. It may be that if we were to carefully study it, a more significant meaning may grow around it in our hearts and change our lives for good.

The first phrase of the first sentence says, "Our Father which art in heaven."

This is the acknowledgment or faith clause. It represents our belief in God and is the foundation upon which everything else rests. Speaking of this great power of faith, Jesus said, ". . . all things are possible to him that believeth." (Mark 9:23.) What glory our lives would manifest if our faith were fully developed and its power utilized by us! In these six short words, we voice the important acknowledgment that we believe in God, that we trust him, and that we understand the kind of being he is. We know what God's ambition is, for he himself has said, ". . . this is my work and my glory—to bring to pass the immortality and eternal life of man." (Moses 1:39.) The life of Jesus was also devoted to this purpose. He referred to his work as "my Father's business," which is the business of building character, godliness, and eternal life into God's children. We know that Jesus was created in the image of his Father's person. He was the First Begotten Son of God in the spirit and the Only Begotten Son of God in the flesh.

The faith clause, "Our Father which art in heaven," is joined naturally with our acceptance and covenant of devotion, which says, "Hallowed be thy name."

That is, we not only know the kind of being that God is and our relationship to him; we also pledge to keep his sacred name holy in our lives.

The second and third sentences combined are only fourteen words long and might well be considered together. The first sentence of three words says, "Thy kingdom come." The second sentence of eleven words says, "Thy will be done in earth as it is in heaven."

This earth and its inhabitants are presently being prepared for better things, and when the earth shall have filled the measure of its creation, it shall become celestialized and glorified to serve as the everlasting abode of those who qualify for God's highest kingdom. The earth is now a telestial sphere; it has existed in its lowest state since the fall of man. But when it is redeemed, it will become a celestial sphere suited for the presence of God himself. In the meantime, it is our job to help make this earth into a heaven.

Nearly two thousand years ago, as Jesus, upon the Mount of Olives, foretold his own glorious second coming to the earth in the last days, he told of the wars and difficulties that would precede his coming. Then he said, "And this gospel of the kingdom shall be preached in all the world, as a witness unto all nations, and then shall the end come." The gospel is now going forth for the last time. When the glorious second coming takes place, the earth will then be temporarily lifted to a terrestrial sphere and Christ will reign here personally during the millennium of a thousand years. During this period of peace, the family of God will be perfected and bound together. Then, following the millennium, the earth will be celestialized and glorified and made fit for the presence of God. When the earth has been redeemed and its inhabitants perfected to become like God, the will of God will be done on the earth, as it is now done in heaven. This is God's final objective for us, and toward this end he has invited all of us to lend our own efforts.

The fourth sentence of the Lord's Prayer says, "Give us this day our daily bread." Certainly God didn't mean that we should receive our living without any effort on our part. Our material as well as our spiritual salvation is brought about as a cooperative enterprise. God intends that we ourselves should help to provide for ourselves. Work is important for our development. It is the process by which our eternal progression is brought about. Even God is God because of what he does. Someone has said:

We serve no God whose work is done,
Who rests within his firmament,
Our God, his work has just begun,
Toils ever more with powers unspent.

It is the natural law of our being that when one becomes inactive mentally, spiritually, or physically, he starts downhill. Thus, God has made planning, industry, and struggle essential for our growth. Earning our bread is like most of the other good things in life: we not only get our bread by our labor, but we learn to do by doing and we develop strength by practice. So sentence number four of the Lord's Prayer is the work sentence, the action clause.

Then, in the fifth sentence, the Lord says, "And forgive us our debts, as we forgive our debtors." This, like all of these other important ideas, is a brief statement summarizing a great natural law. Jesus said, "For if ye forgive men their trespasses, your heavenly Father will also forgive you: But if ye forgive not men their trespasses, neither will your

Father forgive your trespasses." (Matthew 6:14-15.) What a tremendous opportunity this idea presents for us! It is a partial restatement of the Golden Rule. Indirectly, it makes each of us his own judge; but in addition, what a wonderful world we would have if we all proceeded on the basis of forgiveness of others and treating all of our fellowmen as we would like to be treated.

This phrase also indicates that God expects us to answer as many of our own prayers as we are able. That is, what point would there be in asking God to forgive our enemies? We can do that far more effectively ourselves; and if we do not forgive them, God has indicated that he will not forgive us. Or why should we ask God to make us kind, thoughtful, loving, and obedient to him? That is another prayer that he has already given us the power, the authority, and the command to answer.

Many of our blessings are based almost entirely on what we ourselves do. Frequently we bear testimony and voice approval that God hears and answers prayers; but we should also thank him that some of our petitions are declined. Oscar Wilde once said that "if God wished to punish us, all he would need to do would be to answer our prayers." We should thank God that prayer is not merely an effortless ritual that is carried out on our knees; it is also a labor that we perform on our feet.

Above the fireplace in the home of the late Henry Ford was an inscription that said, "He who chops his own wood, warms himself twice." And he who helps to answer his own prayers not only gets the blessing—he gets the strength as well. We may make ourselves just as wise, just as strong, and just as godlike as we desire ourselves to be.

The sixth sentence of the Lord's Prayer begins, "And lead us not into temptation, but deliver us from evil." Here we are reminded of the great law of free agency. God is committed to free agency. If we believe that faith without works is dead, then it naturally follows that the hands that labor in God's work are just as holy as the lips that pray about it. The Lord's Prayer is a prayer of works as well as a prayer of faith.

We live in a world of opposites, in which the extremes of good and evil are always before us. In considering any issue, it would be well for us to walk completely around it so that we can understand both its negative and its positive sides. We should always remember that we are our own masters and must be responsible for the consequences of our own deeds. Certainly one of our greatest privileges is to develop that godlike tendency to avoid evil and to do good.

The climax of the Lord's great prayer comes in the last phrase. This is a summing up, a re-expression of our devotion. It is the benediction and the declaration that we accept God, that he is our Father, that he is all-wise, all-knowing, all-powerful, all-righteous. In him is no shadow of turning. His laws can always be depended upon. Therefore, with heartfelt love and earnest devotion, we say to him, "For thine is the kingdom, and the power, and the glory, for ever."

Index

Money, use of, 212-14
Morale, 209
Mormon Church, name of, 18
Mortal body, 216
Mortality, 2, 135, 160, 205, 217
Moses, 55, 200
Mothers, 190
Motivation, 206
Mount Moriah, 41
Mount of Olives, 12
Mount Sinai, 200

Napoleon, 190
National Gallery of Art, 31
Nebuchadnezzar, 43
Negativism, 97-100, 219
Notebooks of quotations, 30

Obedience, 169, 172
Objectives of life and death, 34
Obstacles, 3
Opposites, 234
Optical illusions, 73

Parables of Jesus, 33, 101, 168, 225
Peace on earth, 167
Pearl Harbor, attack on, 194
Pearl of Great Price, 19
Pecking order, 130
Penitentiary, inmates of, 108
People, importance of, 149
Period, 176
Personality, 91; sins against, 91-95;
    importance of, 95
Perspective, 73-77
Phylacteries, 52
Pilgrims, 164
Pleasure, 54
Point, definitions of, 73; of view, 98
Pope, Alexander, 156
Popenoe, Paul, 180
Positive thinking, 182
Prayer, answer to, 233
Preaching, 62
Preexistence, 135
Preparation, 195-98
Pride, 116
Priesthood, 225, 226
Prisoners, ranking of, 132
Probation, mortal, 87-90
Problems, people with, 49-50, 93, 104,
    113

Procrastination, 99, 177
Procreation, 10
Prodigal son, parable of, 107-108
Prohibition laws, 141
Promises, empty, 170
Protestant reformers, 6
Pump, priming the, 163-67
Punctuation, 174-78
Pure language of God, 177
Purification, 135-39

Qualifying for position, 192
Quarterback, 54
Question marks, 175, 176
Quotation marks, 177

Radiance, inner, 58
Railroad track, 74
Rank, 130-34
Ratings, 130-34
Rationalization, 99
Reasoning power, 8
Rebellion, 202; against authority, 127
Reformation, 218
Rehearsals in life, 199
Repentance, 51, 137, 138, 140-45, 169
Respect for others, 94, 128, 160
Responsibility, 103; personal, 57, 71
Restitution, 140-45
Restoration of Christ's church, 9, 17-
    18
Resurrection, 12-13, 134, 135, 166, 205,
    220, 223
Revelations, 227; modern-day, 20
Righteousness, 48, 58, 138, 215
Roberts, B.H., 151
Roosevelt, Franklin D., 31
Roosevelt, Theodore, 155
Ruskin, John, 177
Ruth, Babe, 157

Sabbath day, 8
Sacrament, 78-83
Sacramental prayer, 82
Salesmanship ideas, 28, 70
Salvation for the dead, 228
Sandburg, Carl, 30
Satan, xiii
Savile, E.S.G., 61
Saving, 211
Science, in 20th century, 18
Scriptures, 180; modern-day, 19;
    books of, 61